DAYTONA U.S.A.

The official history of Daytona and Ormond Beach racing from 1902 to today's NASCAR super speedways.

by William Neely

Foreword
by Bill France, Sr.

Salute
by Bill Mitchell

AZTEX Corporation—Tucson, AZ 85703

Acknowledgments & Credits

I wish to sincerely thank Bill France, Sr., Bill Tuthill and Jim Foster for accepting me back to Daytona, and for their help and faith. This book would not have been possible without them. And also special gratitude to Ron Meade, Mike Joy, Jim Hunter, Donna Freismuth, Jamie Foster, Bob Mauk, Alexis Leras, Dennis Winn, Bob Costanzo, Jim Bockoven, Jackie Arute, Helen Webbe, Tim Flock, Cale Yarborough, Richard Petty, Lee Petty, Fred Messersmith, Daytona International Speedway, NASCAR, Daytona News-Journal and the Ormond Historical Society.

Photo Credits:
Anheuser-Busch
Cummins Diesel
Daytona International Speedway
Detroit Public Library, National Automotive History Collection
General Motors Alumni Association
Glenn Curtiss Museum of Local History
Goodyear News Bureau
Mercedes Benz of North America
Museum of Speed
NASCAR News Bureau
Ormond Beach Historical Society
R. J. Reynolds Tobacco Co.
Teledyne Wisconsin Motor
Union Oil Co.
Valvoline Oil Co.

Cover Art: John M. Peckham
Composition: Text, California 10 pt.; Captions, California 8 pt.
Typesetting: Maria L. Montijo
Color Separations: Color Masters, Inc., Phoenix, Arizona
Printing: RAE Lithographers, Inc., Cedar Grove, New Jersey
Binding: Horowitz & Sons, Fairfield, New Jersey

ISBN 0-89404-005-7 hardbound
ISBN 0-89404-025-1 softbound

Library of Congress Catalog Card Number 79-55462

AZTEX CORPORATION, TUCSON, ARIZONA 85703

Printed in the United States of America

Contents

Appendix
Daytona Records

Foreword

DAYTONA U.S.A. brings to all of us who have grown up in the automotive age many fond memories—starting from the earliest days of motor sports competition at the birthplace of speed in Ormond Beach to the last four mile beach road course at the south end of Daytona Beach. Then on to the new era of speed at the now famous 2-1/2 mile tri-oval banked speedway. The new race course expands to 3.8 miles for the 24 Hour Pepsi Challenge—the sister race to the famous 24 Hour of LeMans.

Daytona has contributed much to the sports scene. The founding of NASCAR, the first live telecast of a road race emceed by the great Walter Cronkite. Bob Osiecki and Art Malone broke the 180 mph mark on the new track after some race officials had said the new speedway was too fast. After Malone's run the Indy type cars were drastically redesigned to utilize negative lift to hold the cars on the ground. While Osiecki and Malone pioneered car design, much credit and mention should go to the initial founders and employees of NASCAR. Bill Tuthill and Anne France—officers of NASCAR, Red Vogt—who came up with the *name* NASCAR. Bob Sall and Ed Otto—who pioneered NASCAR in the north, Millie Ayers—who recorded the founding meeting, Dee Connors, Buddy Shuman, Bill Taylor, Norris Friel—technical directors. Dorothy Beech, Joe Littlejohn, Pat Purcell, Russ Moyer, Judy Jones, Anne Slack, Jane Parker, Clay Earles, Enoch Staley, Alvin Hawkins, Mary Ficacci, Houston Lawing and Jim Foster have all played some part in developing NASCAR into an internationally respected racing organization.

Certainly NASCAR gained stature by the type of men who have served as the Commissioners—E.G. "Cannonball" Baker was the first, then Harley Earl—the distinguished G.M. Vice President and designer. Following Harley was the Honorable L. Mendell Rivers—Chairman of the House Armed Services Committee, and at present the Honorable Semon L. Knudsen—Chairman of White Motor Corporation and life-long automobile and racing enthusiast and sportsman.

When I retired as President of NASCAR in 1972 I felt that NASCAR was in capable hands with Bill France, Jr. and Lin Kuchler heading a competent staff. Bill deserves much credit for expanding NASCAR's operations and developing NASCAR into one of the finest racing organizations in the world today.

Credit should be given to all members of the present NASCAR staff—Jim France as Vice President and Secretary, John Riddle, Bill Gazaway, Bob Smith, Alexis Leras, Doris Rumery, Joe Epton and Bill Tauss.

Special thanks to Bill Neely and Walt Haessner for making this book possible.

I'm proud to have been a part of much that has been recorded in *DAYTONA U.S.A.*

Bill France, Sr.

Dedication

To Martina: At long last, love

A gentle January breeze drifted in from the Halifax River and murmured along the hundred yards or so of porch on the south side of the Ormond Hotel. The porch formed a sort of promonade for guests of the sprawling frame, Victorian resort. A few strolled up and down the cyprus-planked veranda, but most sat in cane-bottomed rocking chairs, their attention focused on a newly-completed garage just up Granada Avenue toward the ocean.

It had become the typical pastime for the scores of wealthy winter guests to rock and watch with great anticipation as *race cars* pulled in and out of the Ormond Garage, American's first "Gasoline Alley" and the birthplace of speed.

Racing had taken hold. "Now is the time," wrote Burr McIntosh in his monthly magazine of 1904. "Automobile racing in the United States is in its infancy. It can be made a tremendously high class sport, or it can fall into the hands of professionalism. Both are all right in their way and should be encouraged, but a close study of events will prove that automobiling will have a very similar career to football. No professional football team was ever made permanently successful...Let us guard this great, big, far-reaching sport in its infancy, so that it may develop into a being, which shall be a constant source of delight, satisfaction and pride to us all."

McIntosh apparently did not know how important automobile racing—and professional football, for that matter—was to become to Americans; otherwise he might have been able to predict that Daytona Beach would become the world center of racing. He might even have predicted that a highly-celebrated speedway would be built there or that the world's premier racing association would take roots in Daytona.

After all, it was inevitable. With 23 miles of smooth, hard beach, it was only a matter of time after the automobile surfaced until somebody came to the beach to use that sandy turnpike for automobile racing.

The first race was held in 1902, but the two men who competed were not ordinary, garden-variety race drivers; they were men of means, fathers of a fledgling industry, owners of companies that *made* cars. They were out of the board rooms and onto the beach in their own creations.

Ransom E. Olds, who gave the world the Oldsmobile and the Reo (consider Olds' initials), was the first man ever to race on the beach in a timed run. He drove his Olds Pirate just over 50 miles per hour, returned to the library at the Ormond Hotel, bubbled enthusiastically to his friend

Part of the crowd that was on hand in 1902 to watch the first race on the beach, the Olds-Winton contest. The sight-seeing bus, left, was the first vehicle sold by Olds.

Alexander Winton, who also owned an automobile company: "You have no idea, Alex," he said, "what a thrill it is out there. Do you know what it feels like to go 50 miles per hour?"

Olds may not have been aware of it, but he had issued the first racing challenge in the history of the beach. History is unclear as to the rest of the conversation, and the two pioneers have been gone for a long time, but it is agreed that they brought racing to the beach. And in splendid fashion.

Later in the season, Olds and Winton breakfasted at dawn in the gracious, columned dining room of the hotel, passing pleasantries and small talk as they had on other mornings. An hour later, they sat patiently in their race cars on Ormond Beach, pointed south toward Daytona Beach, Olds in the Pirate and Winton in the Bullet. The cars rocked and popped and belched puffs of black smoke, as if talking to one another. Olds straightened his necktie and then snapped a salute from the brim of his tweed cap. Winton returned the gesture and the starter dropped the flag.

The cars lurched forward and the crowd of 50 or so spectators cheered politely, not yet overcome with the passion for auto racing that would come in later years.

The Bullet coughed and sputtered for a second and Olds took a slight lead, but Winton pulled alongside as the cars became tiny dots down the beach. A handful of onlookers stood atop the grassy dunes that ran along sandy North Atlantic Avenue, and they waved as the stripped-down race cars zipped past them.

Somewhere down the beach, the cars swung back North, and as they appeared in sight of their starting point, they were again side by side. The drivers pulled to a stop and were again side by side. The drivers pulled to a stop and jumped down from their buckboard seats, proclaiming an absolute tie. They had clocked an impressive 57 miles per hour.

The declaration of a tie assuredly was a mark of the men who raced that first race. And it may well have cast the mold for the romantic figures who were to fly World War I fighter planes, but it certainly never was to be repeated in automobile racing.

Ransom E. Olds in his "Pirate," the first car ever to race on the beach. He attained a speed of over 50 miles per hour in 1902.

Winton, smitten with speed, returned the following year, 1903, with an improved Bullet and zinged through a measured mile at a speed of 68.19 miles per hour—over a mile a minute—beating a host of steam, electric and gasoline-powered cars that had also showed up to race. It was, however, 1904 before the Winter Speed Carnival really got rolling. The Ormond Hotel became the mecca for wealthy sportsmen and society types. It was one of these affluent sportsmen who brought the first world speed record to Ormond Beach. William K. Vanderbilt in a Mercedes roared through the mile at 92.30 miles per hour to eclipse the mark set by Henry Ford in "999" one month earlier on Michigan's frozen Lake St. Clair.

The building of the Ormond Garage coincided with the real action on the beach. Entries poured in from all over the world for the 1905 speed contest. It was a year for many "firsts;" Barney Oldfield took the first step to becoming a household speed word as he raced up and down the beach; Walter Christie entered his front-wheel drive, transverse-mounted engine car (and when told it would never sell, went out and invented the army tank); Henry Ford appeared with a six-cylinder vehicle; the first streamlined automobile, a steam car, was entered by Louis Ross; the first 100 miles per hour mark was recorded; the first fatality was registered, and the very first dispute over rules. It was truly "the week that was."

Bostonian H. L. Bowden, driving a monstrous twin-engined Mercedes, became the first man in America to surpass the 100 mile per hour mark as he roared through the traps at 109.75. But Arthur MacDonald drove his British Napier to a 104.65 mph average, and then promptly protested the Bowden run because his car was "over the weight limit." In perhaps the first example of international racing diplomacy, race officials salvaged American, German and British feelings by crediting *both* Bowden and MacDonald with an "official" speed record.

Frank Crocker, a wealthy New Yorker, sped down the beach at nearly 100 miles per hour and swerved into the surf to avoid a bicyclist. Crocker and his French mechanic died in the crash.

Perhaps it was the Crocker crash, perhaps rising horsepower and speed, but the millionaire sportsmen began to shy away from the driving duties, and the professional race driver came into being in 1906. He did not have

W. K. Vanderbilt, with fur collar and goggles, arrives in Daytona in 1904 with the Mercedes which established a 92 mile per hour record.

Every car in Daytona Beach lined up for this photograph prior to the record runs in 1905.

AMERICA'S FIRST GASOLINE ALLEY...This photo was taken during Speed Week in 1905, the first full week of racing and speed activity held anywhere in the world. The building was built by Henry M. Flagler to house the early day racing creations and was located on Granada Avenue in Ormond Beach, Florida. Tracks in the foreground were for a horse car which carried people to the beach about a quarter mile distant. Granada Avenue also marked the north end of the original racing course.

The first Ford Factory team at Ormond Beach, 1905. Henry Ford, with goggles, drove "666" to a speed of 91 miles per hour on the beach.

The clubhouse and headquarters for the first beach racing speed week of 1903 was located just north of the Silver Beach approach. This 1905 photo shows the number 39 on the front of the building, which indicated the 39 seconds it took W. K. Vanderbilt to cover the measured mile, establishing the first world record on the beach.

immediate first class citizenship, however.

The first professional drivers were little more than hired hands, using the back entrance to the Ormond Hotel, driving their bosses around and, generally, completing any unsavory task that needed doing. The Europeans further distinguished themselves from their drivers by listing only last names for the chauffeurs. Consequently many old records do not indicate a given name.

One in particular, a Frenchman named Hemery, was notorious; he insulted the Italians, snubbed the British, called the Americans "mechanical peasants," and tried to destroy the only car that was faster than his powerful Darracq, which, incidentally, was the first V-8 anybody in Daytona had ever seen. It had overhead valves and hemi heads.

Hemery's only rival for the speed record was a soft-spoken American,

The twin-engined Mercedes of H. L. Bowden ran 109 miles per hour in 1905.

The first drag race in history. In 1905 the Stanley Steamer, with Louis Ross at the wheel, right, easily outran, from left to right, E. R. Thomas and W. K. Vanderbilt in the Mercedes' and H. McDonald in the Napier.

At the 1905 Ormond Beach, Florida automobile races—W. K. Vanderbilt, Jr., in his 90hp Mercedes.

Louis S. Ross's steam automobile making mile record of 38 seconds, Ormond Beach, Florida, 1905.

Fred Marriott, driving the Stanley Steamer. Sensing the potential of the steam car, Hemery pulled alongside the wood and canvas-bodied steamer, positioning his open exhaust stacks so they pointed directly at the side of the American car. And he revved his engine, blacking the sides of the Stanley, but not igniting it as Hemery had hoped. Hemery was disqualified by race officials and fired by the Darracq company. Marriott went on to beat the entire European aggregation by completing the world's first two mile per minute run. He completely exasperated the gasoline people with his 127 mile per hour effort.

The sand was rough for the 1907 meet and drivers waited impatiently for tides to improve the surface. On the final day, Marriott rolled out the Steamer and announced that he would make his run despite the rough conditions. "We'll glide right over the rough spots at top speed," he announced. The boiler of the Stanley was wrapped with more than one mile of piano string to keep it from blowing up under the stress of more than 1000 pounds pressure.

The car was at maximum power as it streaked off the starting line with a blazing acceleration that only steam cars had in those days. He took nine miles to build up to the measured mile, and he was doing an estimated 197 miles per hour as he reached the traps. In fact, he was still accelerating when he hit the rough part of the beach.

The streamlined racer took off, flying directly for the surf. It crashed in a thundering heap one-quarter of a mile from where it had left the sand, strewing parts everywhere. Marriott escaped serious injury, but the accident so shook the Stanley brothers that they gave up all future racing activities, which was the most severe setback to automobile racing in history.

While race officials were still reeling from the spectacular crash, Glenn H. Curtiss appeared with his gargantuan motorcycle, complete with a V-8 engine (keep in mind that it was 1907).

"I wonder if you could time me?" he asked. "I mean, while you still have your timing device in operation."

Startled race officials asked if he had seen what just happened, and he replied, "Yes, but I'm low on funds, you see, and . . ."

In a matter of minutes, Curtiss roared through the traps at 136.30 miles per hour, prompting a headline in the following day's *Chicago Daily News* that read: "Fastest Mile On Earth. Bullets Are the Only Rivals of Glenn Curtiss."

Glenn Curtiss on motorcycle, 1907.

The feat so impressed Alexander Graham Bell that he persuaded Curtiss to join his group, which was pioneering in aircraft power. Curtiss went on to become the first licensed pilot in America and, using the same motorcycle engine, made one of the first official airplane flights in the world. Then he went to Europe and won the first air race in history.

Curtiss continued his aeronautical research and developed flying boats and take-offs and landings on ships, becoming the acknowledged Father of Naval Aviation. Quite a destiny for a young man who at one time had slept beside his motorcycle in the Ormond Garage.

Road racing began to spring up throughout Europe and the United States, so race officials at the beach devised a sort of race "course" to attract the top cars of the world. They placed a flag in the center of the beach at the foot of Granada Avenue in Ormond as the marker for the extreme north end of the course. Twelve and one-half miles south in Daytona, they put up another flag, indicating the other end of the course. The cars simply raced around the flags, completing the 25-mile circuit. It was quite a sight to see

Hemmery in the 200hp Darracq car which made the mile in 30.35 seconds, Ormond Beach, Florida, 1906.

Clifford-Earp in Napier which made five mile record on heavy track in 2 minutes 56 seconds; and the 100 mile in 1 hour, 15 minutes, 3.5 seconds. Ormond Beach, 1906.

Marriott and the Stanley Steamer which made a world's record mile in 28.15 seconds, Ormond Beach, Florida, 1906.

The end of the line for the Stanley Steamer. Fred Marriott was near the 200 mile per hour mark in 1907 when the Steamer became airborne and crashed into the surf, ending the development of the fastest car in the world.

cars roaring up and down the beach, going in different directions on the same straightaway.

Vanderbilt Cup winner George Robertson, veteran Louis Strang in a Buick factory racer and a young sensation named Ralph DePalma in a factory Fiat were the favorites for the first beach course races. Before the three-

*1908—Start of a race to prove the automobile superior to the airplane.
Both started out on a dead start—the automobile won, proving the
airplane would never take the place of a car....*

day meet had ended, each had won a race. It was DePalma, however, who
stole the hearts of the crowd. His Fiat Cyclone won the long-distance
race—an amazing 150 miles. The mere thought of an automobile staying
together for such a distance at speeds over 100 miles per hour astonished
everyone, including most of the drivers.

The race was flagged to a stop a few miles before the finish because of
the incoming tide. DePalma's car was the only one running.

*Emanuel Cerdino, above, drove the Fiat
Cyclone on the beach in 1908. He was later
killed in the same car at the Pimlico,
Maryland, track. The car was repaired and
driven to victory by Ralph DePalma in the
first long-distance race (150 miles) on the
beach.*

It took a 1,300 cubic inch-engined German car to wrest the overall
speed title away from the Stanley Steamer, but there was an American at the
wheel. Barney Oldfield entered the 1910 episode of speed with the Blitzen
Benz and easily surpassed the record, raising it to 131.72. He described the
tremendous acceleration of the Benz as "the sensation of riding a rocket
through space." Proving himself more of a race driver than prophet, he
added: "A speed of 131 miles an hour is as near to the absolute limit of speed
as humanity will ever travel."

1300 cu. in. powerplant for the Blitzen Benz.

Barney Oldfield at the wheel of the Blitzen (Lightning) Benz which he drove 131 miles per hour in 1910.

Oldfield, with his ever-present cigar, was the speed king of the world. He even received a congratulatory telegram from Kaiser William II of Germany.

The following year Oldfield was replaced in the Benz by Bob Burman. Oldfield was still convinced that he had achieved the pinnacle of speed. But Burman's talents were quickly displayed in practice runs that were so fast that the lenses of his racing goggles were repeatedly blown from the frames. Undaunted, Burman simply riveted the lenses to the frames and celebrated

BENZ

AUTOMOBILE

BENZ & Cᴵᴱ

Rheinische Gasmotoren-Fabrik Aktiengesellschaft

MANNHEIM

Telegramm-Adresse: Benzwerke Mannheim
Telephon: Nr. 6545, 6546, 6547, 6548
Telegraphenschlüssel: A.B.C. 5th Edition, Staudt & Hundius
Lieber's Engineering Code 2nd Edition
Whitelaw's 407, 600 Words, Private Code

Zweigniederlassungen in Deutschland:
Hamburg · Bremen · Dortmund · Essen (Ruhr) · Düsseldorf · Köln · Koblenz · Straßburg
Stuttgart · Nürnberg · Plauen i.Vogtld. · Chemnitz · Leipzig · Dresden · Breslau · Kattowitz
Posen · Stettin · Rostock.

Vertretungen in Deutschland:
Berlin · Königsberg i.Pr. · Magdeburg · Hannover · Braunschweig · Osnabrück · Erfurt
Frankfurt a.M. · München · Mannheim · Karlsruhe · Saarbrücken.

Ausländische Gesellschaften:
Automobiles BENZ (Société Anonyme) 10, Avenue Bugeaud, Paris
BENZ Motors Limited, 78, Brompton-Road, London S.W.
Österreichische BENZ-Motoren-Gesellschaft m.b.H., Kämmerring 14, Wien I
Magyar BENZ Automobilgyár R.-T., Ilka-utcza 31, Budapest
Russische Automobil- und Motoren-Aktiengesellschaft, Newski Prospekt 57, St. Petersburg
BENZ Auto Import Company of America, 244, 246, 248, West 54th Street, New York.

200 P.S. BENZ-RENNWAGEN

auf dem Bob Burman den bisher von Benz gehaltenen Weltrekord von
212 Kilometer überboten hat, indem er bei fliegendem Start in Daytona
(Florida) am 23.April 1911 eine Geschwindigkeit von

228 Kilometer in der Stunde

erreichte und somit einen neuen

WELTREKORD

aufstellte.

Die Schnelligkeit, Zuverlässigkeit und Dauerhaftigkeit der Benz-Automobile
sind das Ergebnis gründlich durchgeprobter und 25 jähriger Erfahrungen im
Automobilbau, praktisch verwertender Konstruktion in Gemeinschaft mit
solidester und gewissenhaftester Präzisionsarbeit unter Verwendung allerbesten
Materials.

Wir bauen:

TOURENWAGEN	STADTWAGEN
GESCHÄFTSWAGEN	LASTFAHRZEUGE
MOTORDROSCHKEN	MOTOROMNIBUSSE
FEUERSPRITZEN	MANNSCHAFTSWAGEN
RETTUNGSWAGEN etc.	

Unsere Abteilung MOTORENBAU liefert:
Rohölmotoren (System Diesel) für stationäre und Schiffszwecke. Gasmotoren. Benzin-
motoren. Benzolmotoren. Petroleummotoren. Sauggasanlagen für Anthrazit. Braun-
kohlenbriketts. Holzkohlen und Torf. Fahrbare Motoren mit Baumaschinen. Bandsägen.
Beleuchtungswagen.

Kataloge und Preislisten stehen Interessenten bereitwilligst zu Diensten.

Daytona Beach racing had world-wide marketing impact on the fledgling automotive business. This 1911 Benz catalog makes use of Bob   *Burman's speed record on the sands.*

Burman's speed was so intimidating that it discouraged anyone from even trying to break it for the next eight years. It was considered unbreakable. That is until America's supreme racing hero, Ralph DePalma, returned in 1919 with the most impressive array of victories in history. Since his last trip to the beach, DePalma had won the Indianapolis 500, the Vanderbilt Cup, the national driving championship and more than one hundred races. He was considered by most to be the greatest race driver who ever lived.

DePalma was not only anxious to break the record of the Benz, but to do it with an American-made machine. His long, torpedo-shaped racer was powered by a newly-designed V-12 Packard engine with a displacement of 905 cubic inches. The fierce engine had set records in the air and in Gar Wood's speedboats. And DePalma had won several automobile races with the power plant. Packard wanted to add the world land speed record to its

Ralph De Palma in Packard 12-cylinder, powered by second airplane prototype engine, 905cc, Daytona, February 12, 1919.

Ralph DePalma in the V-12 Packard which established every world record in 1919 from one to twenty miles, including a standing start mark that was not broken until 1955.

list of accomplishments. The gracious DePalma matter-of-factly climbed in, waved to the crowd, and roared down the beach at 149.87 miles per hour.

DePalma, who already held nearly every American speed mark, stayed at the beach for another week, methodically breaking every world mark, from two to 20 miles. He was ready to depart, holding every speed mark anyone could think of—or any combination—when someone remembered Oldfield's standing start mark of 88.84 mph, which had been set eight years earlier. DePalma said, "Well, lads, we can't go home yet," and he climbed back in the big Packard and made one more trip through the traps—at 92.71 miles per hour.

"Now, we can go home," he said.

The standing start record, although partially over-shadowed by future all out speed runs, stood for 36 years, and it took a V-12 Ferrari to break the mark in 1955. The Ferrari record was significant because the memoirs of Enzo Ferrari included this paragraph: "Just after World War I, I had the occasion to see the 12-cylinder engine of the magnificent Packard. I always

liked the song of 12 cylinders; what is more, I must confess that the fact that there was only one firm in the world making such engines acted on me as a challenge and a spur. When Packard abandoned their 12-cylinder engine, then I was the only one making them."

Tommy Milton, whose fervent desire was to take away the "Number One" title from DePalma, arrived at the Ormond Garage in 1920 with one of the most advanced racing machines of the period. Milton had handled almost every detail of the streamliner, which featured a slanting nose and long tail section. Under the hood of the sleek racer were two Duesenberg engines, mounted side by side.

There were still a few minor details that needed looking after when Milton arrived, but he left them to his mechanic, Jimmy Murphy, and he headed on to Cuba to drive in a race. Milton was stunned upon his return when he learned that Murphy had not only completed the car, but had driven it to a new speed record of more than 152 miles per hour. He fired Murphy on the spot and took the twin Duesenberg to the beach himself, only to find that the sand and salt from Murphy's runs had damaged the engines. Milton couldn't get near the Murphy record.

Milton, driven by as much steam as the Stanley brothers' race car of an earlier era, tore down the engines and completely rebuilt them, preparing for his turn at the record. He had no idea how exciting it was going to be.

Halfway through the measured mile, flames began to leap through the hood louvers, but Milton scrunched down in his seat a little more and he held his foot to the floor. The car streaked through the timing traps, the front end engulfed in flames. Milton steered as close to the surf as he dared, hoping the spray would extinguish the flames. The crowd gasped. As the car slowed down, the flames turned to smoke and finally all trace of the fire was gone. The huge throng cheered wildly as Milton alighted from the car. They roared even louder when his speed was announced—156.046 miles per hour. Tommy Milton was the world's record holder.

It was certainly not the last anyone would hear of Tommy Milton. He won the Indianapolis 500 in 1921 and 1923. Jimmy Murphy won the 500 in 1922.

The next record on the beach was unofficial, although all who were present quickly attested to its authenticity. Sig Haugdahl, who was a member of the International Motor Contest Board, a rival sanctioning body to the American Automobile Association, the official timing body for beach runs, arrived at the beach with a white, torpedo-shaped car, powered by a modified Wisconsin aircraft engine.

IMCB had certified the electrical timing device before and after the run. They surveyed the measured mile to avoid any possible criticism. And, as an added precaution, they brought along as official observers a United States Senator and the Mayor of Daytona Beach. Politicians obviously had a different image in those days.

The 1920 record car of Tommy Milton was powered by two four-cylinder Duesenberg engines, and was the first racing car with a windshield and headrest. Milton, two-time Indy 500 winner, established a record of 156.046 in the car.

Sig Haugdahl in the Wisconsin Special.

Although the mark was not included in most record books, Haugdahl was clocked at 180.27 miles per hour—the world's first three mile per minute run.

In 1927, Major H. O. D. Seagrave opened a period of nearly total British domination that was to last as long as the land speed record runs themselves at the beach. Seagrave brought the most costly and most secretive entry in the quarter-century of racing at Daytona. Arrangements were so well-guarded that Seagrave had arrived in Jacksonville before anyone even knew of his plans to run for the record that year.

He was driven to Daytona, where he checked into what is now the Daytona Plaza Hotel, hoping to keep his presence as quiet as possible. But word leaked out, and there was a sizable welcoming committee on hand when the huge, wooden-crated Sunbeam race car arrived a few days later. At the reception, Seagrave reluctantly announced that he would run the twin aircraft-engined, 1,000 horsepower car for an internationally certified record, which meant that he must make two runs, one in each direction, within a single hour. It was necessary for the international mark to be official.

Major Seagrave became the first man to go over 200 miles per hour in the awsome Mystery S in 1927. The car was powered by twin V-12 aircraft engines, mounted fore and aft of the driver.

Vast crowds showed up for early land speed record runs on the beach and, when there was no official activity, they drove up and down the famous course themselves.

A bathing beauty was on hand to christen the wooden crate which contained the Mystery S car of Major Seagrave.

Seagrave also announced that he planned to break the 200 mile per hour mark, a feat that was hard to comprehend by most because few *airplanes* of that day would go that fast.

The agreeable Irishman explained that his car, the Mystery S, had been engineered specifically for the beach straightaway, and was heavy enough at four tons to be stable, and streamlined enough to cut the wind resistance. Sleek enough to run 212 miles per hour, he reckoned.

Daytona was in the world spotlight as wire service stories poured out daily about the Mystery S. The car remained in the crate and was hauled through the streets of Daytona in parades to stir up even more interest. A bathing beauty christened the crate with a bottle of champagne. The anticipation was almost too much for the seasoned race fans of Daytona.

The crowd was breathless as workmen finally pried off the boards at the end of the crate. A huge cheer went up as the monstrous, red machine was slowly wheeled out. It was both beautiful and awesome-looking. After examining it, few doubted Seagrave's estimated top speed. It was an impressive machine.

Because of the two-way run, the measured mile had to be moved halfway between the Main Street Pier and the inlet. On the morning of March 29, fire sirens told everybody in Daytona that the Mystery S was ready to race. Old-timers say that nearly everybody in Daytona was on hand for the runs, and a world-wide press corps was there to record the event.

Beach entrances were closed, and flags marked the course.

There was little delay in getting it all started. The car had been carefully checked that morning, so Seagrave casually climbed in and adjusted the leather helmet that would, from that point on, bear his name. He fired the first engine, and then the second one. They coughed and sputtered. They finally smoothed out, and the tremendous crowd stood silent as he rolled the Mystery S onto the course.

He made a single practice run to the south and wheeled the car in position for his first official attempt. The timing device was ready. Seagrave was ready. Black smoke poured from the exhausts as he blazed through the traps. At the north end of the beach, Seagrave turned the car around and climbed

Three-time Indianapolis winner Wilbur Shaw drove the Whippet race car to a class record on the beach in 1927.

out. He checked the tires and changed his goggles. And he nodded to the course officials.

Again the engines fired, and Seagrave was on his way, roaring south toward the inlet. By the time Seagrave returned to the timing stand, the results were announced. He had averaged 203.97 miles per hour.

It was only after the second run that he allowed anyone to look at the mysteries of the Mystery S. Each part of the car, he pointed out, had been machined and assembled with such precise accuracy that there was little chance of malfunction. There was no vibration. No problems. An incredible feat, considering the complexity of the engines which were, he revealed, two V-12 aircraft engines that displaced a total of 2,738 cubic inches. One was mounted in front of the driver and one in back. Compressed air started the rear engine which, in turn, started the front one through a friction drive. They were locked together by a common clutch and driven through a three-speed gearbox and countershafts to chains and sprockets on the wheels. It all worked so precisely that Seagrave required but one practice run and two timed runs. It was feat a that was seldom duplicated.

The following year, 1928, saw the most fierce speed battle in Daytona's history. Capt. Malcolm Campbell, a slender millionaire sportsman from England, arrived with his 1,464 cubic inch Napier aircraft-engined Bluebird and the crowds proclaimed "shades of Seagrave" as they watched the streamlined giant being rolled onto the sand. Then came the season's first American challenger, Frank Lockhart, the first rookie ever to win the Indianapolis 500. Lockhart's small, sleek Stutz Blackhawk was a product of his own genius, and probably the most beautiful car ever to run on the beach.

Frank Lockhart in the Stutz Black Hawk Special.

The Blackhawk—which, incidentally, was painted white—was powered by a V-16 engine of only 182 cubic inches, but it developed more than 500 twin-supercharged horsepower. It had been named Stutz Blackhawk after the company that had invested $50,000 in its manufacture. But the costs had greatly exceeded that figure and Lockhart was in debt when he arrived.

The third machine was crude but powerful. The White Triplex was a product of Philadelphian Jim White, whose formula for speed was built around brute force, hence the three Liberty aircraft engines mounted on a chassis of steel railroad tracks. Indianapolis veteran Ray Keech was selected as the Triplex driver.

The salt was rough and finally called "unsuitable" by the course officials. But Campbell elected to practice. Unfortunately the rough surface

The mighty Triplex, powered by three Liberty aircraft engines, roared to a mark of 207 miles per hour with Indy winner Ray Keech at the wheel. Lee Bible was killed in the car the following year.

caused him to crash. Campbell was uninjured so he and his crew began the task of repairing the Bluebird.

Four days of tides had not improved the situation and the sand was still rough when the Bluebird was completed, but Campbell chose again to run. This time, although bounced and battered on his runs, he managed to tie two bruising trips together for a 206.96 mile per hour record.

Lockhart waited three more days before bringing his sleek, lightweight Blackhawk onto the course. The beach was a little better, but still not what officials termed "safe." Lockhart had no choice; he was short on funds, so he decided to run. It was a decision that almost cost him his life. The Blackhawk roared down the beach and emerged from a dense fog bank at the measured mile. The hugh crowd watched in stunned silence when Lockhart veered to the left and hit a soft spot in the sand that catapulted the car end over end into the surf. It landed rightside up but a dazed Lockhart signaled that he was alive, although badly shaken. Spectators rushed to his aid and pulled the car from the surf with Lockhart still behind the wheel.

The rise and fall of the Blackhawk. Frank Lockhart, America's premier racing hero of the late 20s, designed and built the beautiful Stutz Blackhawk, which streaked to a record 198 miles per hour. In an attempt to increase the record. Lockhart flipped the car into the surf.

Spectators rushed to his aid, pulling the car from the tide and perhaps saving the stunned driver from drowning. The car, badly damaged, was returned to Indianapolis to be rebuilt.

A patched-up Lockhart and a battered car returned to Indianapolis, but only after announcing that he would be back.

It was an apprehensive Keech that stayed on to run the Triplex. And brave. During the course of the next few days, Keech was scalded when a hose connection broke; he was overcome by exhaust fumes, and burned when the front engine caught fire; little wonder these things were happening to a driver sitting between a total of 5,000 cubic inches of noise, smoke and vibration. But Keech stayed with it and finally got all three engines running in unison, streaking to a 207.55 mph record.

Officials thought the frantic 1928 season had ended, but Lockhart returned with the rebuilt Blackhawk. He was ready to break the record so he checked all details, leaving only one thing to chance.

America's great racing hero and car-builder, Frank Lockhart, who was fatally injured in the Stutz Blackhawk on the beach in 1928.

Campbell, who had taken a liking to the personable American youth, had warned him to always replace all tires after each run. Lockhart, driven by haste and a lack of funds, ignored the Britisher's advice. His first run was a good one—198 plus—and if he could back it up with a run of say 220 he would hold the record. He had not used full power on the first run, so he was confident as they turned the car around and headed it back down the salt. He elected not to change tires.

He approached the measured mile faster than any man had ever traveled, but he didn't reach the end of the mile. A sickening explosion pierced the early morning air as the right rear tire exploded. The engine was still screaming as the car was thrown completely sideways and began a horrifying 1000-foot roll down the beach. It rolled and flipped time after time, throwing Lockhart onto the sand on the final roll. America's brightest young racing hero and one of its finest car-builders was dead at the age of 26.

The season of 1929 lasted only two days but it was as exciting as any *week* had ever been.

Major Seagrave opened the season with a stunning new car. His Golden Arrow had a low, chiseled nose and gleaming metal panels that covered a 12 cylinder Napier aircraft engine that boasted the unusual arrangement of three banks of four cylinders, sort of like adding an extra bank in the valley

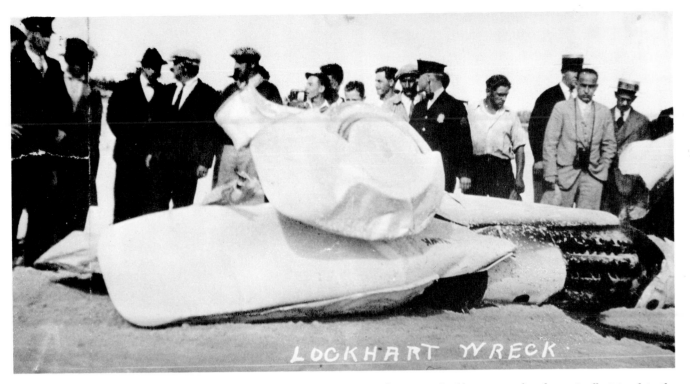

LOCKHART WRECK

Later in the season, Lockhart returned and was fatally injured in the Blackhawk.

of a V-8 engine. Seagrave had proven before that he was a man of action, so when he told the press that the car was designed not only to beat the Triplex record but to become the first four-mile per minute car, nobody questioned.

The beach was rated only "fair," but Seagrave, as he had done before, wheeled his stunning car onto the beach and simply upped the world land speed record to 231.36 mph. Confident of a 240 mile per hour run, he put the car away to wait for the salt to improve—and to watch the runs of the Triplex.

Major Seagrave's "Golden Arrow."

Lee Bible at Daytona Beach, posing in front of the Triplex by White. He
was killed 20 minutes later during his fatal 1929 run.

Ray Keech, who had been paid handsomely the year before for driving
the ferocious Triplex, sent word that he was busy preparing a car for the Indianapolis 500—which he won that year—and, "besides," he had said,
"there's not enough money to get me back in that hot seat."

White arranged for Daytona garage operator Lee Bible to drive the car,
and practice runs proved to officials that he was capable of handling the
earth-shattering machine. It was on the second, and final, day of the racing
meet that Bible rumbled onto the course for the second run.

Bible roared down the beach with a 30-foot rooster tail of sand and salt
spraying up behind. The run looked as if it might be a record, but suddenly
the car swerved out of control. It slid sideways violently and the front
suspension broke, sending the car into a series of cartwheels. A newsreel
photographer, who was stationed in the dunes, panicked and ran directly into the path of the car, which crushed him. When the car stopped high in the
dunes, there were parts strewn all over the beach. And Lee Bible was dead.

The remains of the Triplex in which Lee
Bible lost his life in 1929. Ray Keech, Indianapolis 500 winner, had broken the
record the year before with a 207 mile per
hour run.

Seagrave, who held the record anyway, decided against trying for the 240 mile per hour mark, partly from good judgement and partly out of respect for Bible. But, in an act of the extreme class that had come to be associated with him, he dipped into another gigantic crate that had accompanied the Golden Arrow, and unveiled a large, white speedboat named "Miss England." It was as stunning as his car and he lost no time in getting the Napier engine going. Then he announced that he had retired from automobile racing and would switch to boats. He headed for the Halifax River, where the gleaming white craft thrilled all who moved from the beach side of the peninsula to the river side.

Miss England was a radical departure from the massive boats Gar Wood had raced. Instead, the Seagrave boat weighed only 640 pounds without the engine, which, when installed, was mounted in an unusual position—behind the driver. It turned an unprecedented 6,500 rpm. But the most unusual safety feature was its buoyancy, achieved by filling the hull with thousands of ping pong balls.

Seagrave went off to Miami to race Wood and his Miss America, but it was not until he returned to England that he broke Wood's straightaway record, becoming the first man in history to hold both the land and water world speed marks. Major Seagrave was knighted by King George V of England for his daring accomplishments.

The first winter of the Depression saw speed weeks opening with an appropriately-designed economy vehicle. The Cummins Company had fitted a stock Packard chassis with one of their diesel engines and ended a 3,000-mile tour—which was accomplished on $1.38 worth of kerosene—with an 80 mph run on the beach. It was something less than exciting, but it was the first diesel record.

Nineteen-thirty was not without glamour on the beach, however. Sunbeam entered the fracas again, sending an impressive 31-foot long race car from England. Kaye Don, the British racing star, was selected to drive the Silver Bullet, and he was confident, as were the designers, of a 250 mile per hour run.

The Sunbeam Silver Bullet was one of the most stunning and certainly the longest to compete for the land speed record. Kaye Don, the British racing hero, was unable to break the Seagrave record in the 1930 run, settling for 197 miles per hour.

Kaye Don proved to the world that he was an outstanding driver, just by not killing himself in the car. Or ever crashing. The car was powered by a pair of supercharged V-12 Sunbeam engines mounted in tandem and had a good power-to-weight ratio. But the handling was so bad that the car swerved and veered and bounced down the beach. Spectators, expecting disaster at any moment, stood farther away from the course than they ever had.

Don got the car over 190 mph once, but, after several runs, wisely decided to call it quits. Despite the best beach conditions in years, the car was crated up and returned to England and Kaye Don considered himself lucky to be going back in one piece.

Nineteen-thirty-one action began with another diesel, this time in the chassis of a race car. And this time, with designer-builder Clessie Cummins at the wheel, it became the first diesel to travel over 100 miles per hour. But the diesel run, and subsequent runs by a team of Chryslers that added eight stock car records, were merely preliminary bouts before the main event—the arrival of Malcolm Campbell and his *new* Bluebird.

The Cummins Diesel-Duesenberg that established a record of 100.755 mph at Daytona Beach, February, 1931. This same car was qualified for the 1931 Indianapolis 500 and ran the race non-stop.

The Packard roadster in which Clessie Cummins set the first diesel auto speed record of 80.389 mph, March 20, 1930, at Daytona Beach.

Campbell had been working on plans to break the elusive 240 mile per hour mark. Seagrave had been killed in the crash of Miss England in an attempt to raise the world water speed record, and Campbell, with his gallant rival gone, felt that he was the only one left who could make it.

He proved himself right with a run of 245.73 mph in the new, lower-profile Bluebird. A centrifugal blower boosted the power of the Napier to 1,350 horsepower.

Campbell shocked the racing world by returning in 1932 in an attempt to raise his own record. Experts feared that speeds were already so high that the run would end in disaster. But Campbell—who was now Sir Malcolm, having been knighted for his previous contributions to the science of engineering and high speed—assured the press that the Bluebird was perfectly safe and that the sand was prime for a new record run.

The wind was high on the morning of the run and the flags along the beach danced merrily as Campbell eased into the cockpit of the big blue car. As effortlessly as Seagrave had done it, Campbell streaked across the beach for a two-way average of 253.97 miles per hour. The record was 17

Major Seagrave streaks to a 231 mile per hour record in 1929 in the Golden Arrow despite a rapidly incoming tide.

miles an hour faster than the airplane record set that year in the Thompson Trophy Race.

Campbell astonished the world even further at this farewell party, when he announced that he would return the following year with a goal of 300 miles per hour.

The rest of the land speed record story was all Sir Malcolm Campbell. There would never again be a serious challenger on the beach at Daytona or Ormond other than the quiet, serious-minded Britisher. And Campbell, whose vast fortune came from family holdings in diamond mines, spent money in a fashion that astounded a depression-ridden United States. A United Press story by the late Henry McLemore stated that:

> One hundred thousand dollars is the price Sir Malcolm Campbell will pay for the privilege of risking his neck on the wave-packed sands of Daytona Beach.
>
> The $100,000 represents the cost of outfitting the 1933 venture and ii will come out of his own pocket, too. Sir Malcolm has no backers, (he) does not make his runs as an advertising stunt for any firm. When the mighty Bluebird roars down the beach it roars solely for the honor of Sir Malcolm and the Union Jack.
>
> It was Sir Malcolm who put up the check of many, many thousands

for the Bluebird's new 2,500 horsepower insides, who footed the bill for the transportation of the car, and its mechanics to this country and who, when the runs are completed, will see that everybody gets home again.

Sir Malcolm's runs down the beach this year aren't going to be surrounded by the trimmings of past years. Daytona Beach, like Saulk Center and New York, is finding ready money scarce. Back in the lush days the city thought nothing of rounding up fifteen or twenty thousand dollars to defray the costs of policing, timing and other incidentals.

This year, although the sum they are trying to raise is decidedly less than that, it's been something of a task. The city fathers are holding prize fights, with fifty percent of the gate receipts for the racing fund. Buttons, with pictures of Sir Malcolm and the Bluebird, are 25 cents. Covering the front of the garage where the Bluebird is quartered is a soft drink, cigarette and candy concession and all its intake goes to the fund.

But what about the personal side of this man who was so vital to the development of Daytona as the eventual world center of speed? There was only one other man, a service station operator turned race driver, who contributed as much and fortunately for Daytona, he was to come along near the end of the Campbell era, and will be covered further down the Daytona racing road. But in 1933, here is what Thomas H. Wisdom, morning editor of the London Daily Herald had to say about Sir Malcolm:

Except for those piercing blue eyes, characteristic of lovers of speed, he looks the typical 'gentleman farmer.' Meet him as I have at his beautiful old Elizabethan home near Horley in Surrey, surrounded by his dogs, teaching his son to shoot, walking along country lanes with his daughter and then you have no speed-king, no hunter after buried treasure.

He fits the part—his beautiful home, its valuable collection of antique furniture and the beautiful gardens are not the association one expects of a speed king. Both he and Lady Campbell are enthusiastic gardners. The nine-hole golf course, the pride of his home at Povey Cross, was laid out by Sir Malcolm himself. So was the cinder track on which Donald and Jean, his two youngsters, seek to emulate father by setting new lap records on racing bicycles.

If you look around a little farther at Povey Cross you will penetrate the disguise of Britain's speed-king. There is the glass case, the size of a room, packed with gold and silver trophies of the speed chase. And there is his enormous garage; the last time I was there it held seven cars, ranging from a Rolls-Royce to a 100 mph sports Aston-Martin, all of them painted in the familiar shade of 'Bluebird' blue.

There the adventurer peeps out. Any day you may find him hard at it in his workshop, covered in oil, making something for his cars, his yachts or his children. He motors because he likes motoring. Day after day on the road through Reigate to London a sleek blue car will flash by, faultlessly driven (by) Sir Malcolm on his way to his office.

Day and night his home is guarded by a dozen fierce Alsatian dogs—so fierce that they know and obey but one person—Malcolm himself. Fortunately they are on a chain attached to a wire which goes right around the house.

Continuously these big dogs circle the home, and, without permission, no one dares approach the place. Considering the tremendous value of his trophies and antiques Campbell is right when he says his dogs are his 'best burglary insurance.'

Malcolm Campbell is an adventurer—a modern Drake of Raleigh. He told me once he would like to have been a pirate if he had lived at the right age! Parry, Thomas, Seagrave, Lockhart were all of the same type.

His quest for speed and yet more speed is this inborn sense of adventure expressing itself. He does not make money out of it—no man living has spent more on building costly cars than he, giant machines with their useful life measured in mere seconds. He admitted once that if ever he were persuaded to make out a balance sheet of his countless records bids, he would be the most unhappy man living.

But he goes on. Now his ambition is to exceed 300 mph. He will achieve this and then . . . He says he will retire, but we who know him also know that he will never stop. Many of us would like him to stop. He has done more than his share in this speed-quest. But adventure is life itself to him.

He did not go to Daytona last year. Bluebird was not ready. So, instead he went to Africa in search of buried gold reef in a desert. His companion had to fly back to the base and left Campbell with one bottle of water and an automatic pistol to await his return. 'An uncomfortable couple of days, with the nights the worst' Campbell said when he was rescued eventually. All night he had been surrounded by wild animals. He did not find the gold—the reef was buried under millions of tons of sand. But, if the truth must be told, it was not so much the gold our friend was after—it was the adventure.

It was the same with him always. He likes yachting best when the sea is rough. Never is he so happy as when, during the annual London to Cowes race, the weather in the Channel turns rough, as it usually does. Whether he is at the wheel or frying sausages on the galley stove for his amateur crew he is just as happy.

Malcolm Campbell is 48 years of age, past the age when, so they say, the racing motorist is at his best. He must be the exception that proves the rule. No man has crammed so much adventure, so many narrow escapes, into his life as Sir Malcolm Campbell.

He dislikes being a spectator—that is why he is rarely seen at Brookland's, Britain's chief speedway, except when he is actually competing.

He is superstitious, though he pretends not to be. But he dislikes the number 13, does not regard Friday as a good day for racing and refuses to walk under ladders.

But 'omens' he takes no notice of at all. In one of his early races he opened the shed where his racing car had been garaged to find a hearse neatly drawn up alongside it. Some half-wit pointed out that he would probably be using both vehicles that day. He went out and won the race.

Nothing deters him—he insists on completing every 'job.' At Fanoe Islands, Denmark, back in 1924, he was attempting to beat the record which stood at some 150 miles an hour. Tyres were not so good in those days, and, at full speed a tyre left the wheel and shot on in front of the car. 'Bluebird' skidded broadside on for five miles—a narrow escape in a career packed with escapes from certain death.

Next day Campbell fitted new tyres and went out again—beat the record and then had it disallowed because the electrical timing apparatus had not been approved by the powers that be.

Although he has sought the world speed record at various points all over the world—as have his opponents—Campbell's speed career has been full of similar disappointments until he went to Daytona. He says that Daytona Beach is 'his' course.

His colleagues of the British Racing Drivers Club (of which the author himself was a member) and the 'hero-worshipping' British public, wish that he shall have similar good luck at Daytona this February.

Campbell's presence was of such enormity that everyone wished him good luck, even one of America's first great racing idols, Barney Oldfield, who said:

I would like to add my good wishes to the thousands from all over the world for the accomplishment of the 300 miles per hour speed which Sir Malcolm Campbell hopes to attain on Daytona Beach this year.

Being the first man to turn a one-mile track in 60 seconds—a mile a minute—on that day in 1902, and subsequently establishing and breaking nearly every track record in the early days of racing in the United States, I have a peculiar interest and understanding in Sir Malcolm's speed trials.

People often ask me if I could drive at high speeds today, and I always tell them that I can drive just as fast as I ever drove, but that isn't fast enough. However, I will qualify that statement by saying that I believe it takes a driver of more mature years and the judgment which comes with those years to attain really phenomenal speeds on land.

As I look back upon the days when I became the first man to turn the track in 60 seconds, I wonder and marvel at the accomplishments. My car—old '999'—was a 4 cylinder, 7 inch bore, 7 inch stroke affair with no crankcase, no differential, no rear springs, a direct 1/1 steering ratio, Tiller type—and with a lot of other drawbacks. The car in which I traveled over 131 miles per hour on Daytona Beach in 1910 was not a tremendous improvement over old '999'—except that it went more than twice as fast.

Traveling 300 miles per hour, however, is something new for land vehicles, and it is more than possible that the findings resultant from Sir Malcolm's beautifully streamlined Bluebird may have a direct influence and bearing on the motor car of the future.

Again I say 'Good luck to you, Sir Malcolm, and may you burn up the sands at Daytona Beach!'

Barney Oldfield, left, with his ever-present cigar, wishes "good luck" to Sir Malcolm Campbell before one of his record runs.

Bill Tuthill, who was curator of the Museum of Speed during all of its existence in Daytona, and who is one of America's foremost authorities on speed, was there for the 1933 run by Sir Malcolm Campbell. He describes it this way in his book *Speed on Sand:*

I was among the many thousands here that year. My wife and I had *driven down from New York with a bankroll of $105 and still had twenty left when we returned home almost three weeks later. Mere money, however, could not buy access to the inner sanctum or a detailed explanation of just what made the mighty Bluebird click. But we were there and crew chief Leo Villa was our personal guide.*

...We saw...the engine and everything else that propelled the world's most famous car. And those amazing tires—perfectly smooth, a paper-thin coating of rubber holding together eighteen plies of silk and cotton cord. They cost $1800 each and had a life of only seven minutes, and there were stacks of them. And containers of water for the cooling system shipped all the way from England.

We were introduced to the crew members...Before parting I asked another question: 'This is an automobile but these fellows are aircraft mechanics. Why?'

Crew chief Villa replied that the new Rolls-Royce engine was being developed for the British Air Ministry. And speed records resulting, while incidental really, would add to British prestige.

But, despite the fanatical desire of Campbell to break the 300 mile per hour mark, it was not to be an easy task. The 1933 version of the Bluebird was not prepared for the tremendous output of the Rolls-Royce engine and he was plagued with mechanical problems during his entire stay in America. The best he could do was add about 20 miles an hour to his 1932 record, bringing it to 272.108 miles per hour. Campbell, who had been on the verge of disaster on each run returned to England to better prepare the car for the phenomenal horsepower and torque of the Rolls engine.

The task took two years. "Many of its design features were so far ahead that they were copied extensively for many years, and still are," says Tuthill. "The streamlined nose section of the Dodge Daytona stock racing car introduced in 1969 could have been inspired by the Bluebird. A news release on the 1969 Indianapolis 500 told about the Lotus-Ford entered by English designer Colin Chapman as follows: 'This year Chapman has added new aerodynamic tricks. Air, which rushes through the radiator, leaves the car through a wide slot on top of the nose to increase down force.' New? The Bluebird was built that way in 1935. And Campbell went a step further. At peak speed, approaching the measured mile, he could pull a lever in the cockpit which snapped shut that four-inch opening across the nose and gained an additional 12 miles an hour.

"The high stabilizing fin was later incorporated into many other speed creations, including world record speedboats. In the field of aviation, the wind-breaking air flaps that first appeared on the 707 jet are similar to those built into the Bluebird."

From nose to tail, the thirty foot long body shell built around the five tons of complicated machinery was an outstanding example of the art of aerodynamics. Cam towers on the 2,227 cubic inch V-12 engine were formed into the hood fairing. The entire body and the tail fin were offset and the wheelbase on one side of the car was shorter than on the other to compensate for the tremendous engine torque which otherwise would not permit driving a straight course.

An air scoop in the nose section added a ram effect, boosting air velocity into the big supercharger which forced the fuel mixture into a carburetor almost as large as a complete Volkswagen engine. Its pair of five and one-half inch venturis were fed by a gas line that measured almost two inches in diameter. At full boost, the six-inch pistons churned up 3,500 revs a minute and pushed out 2,700 horses at Daytona's sea level.

Pegged on the tachometer's red line, the engine had a life of only three minutes. Campbell shifted out of low gear at 170, and from second to high at 240 mph.

But, despite the incredible amount of time, engineering and money spent on the project, it seemed to be doomed to disappointment. Even with the dual rear wheels, there seemed to be no way to satisfactorily transfer the phenomenal horsepower to the rear wheels without some sidespinning effect to the five-ton car.

In Campbell's first record run, the car went into a broadslide at 275 miles per hour, tearing the tires to shreds. Campbell was as determined as he was brave. He ordered another set of tires mounted and roared back up the salt. This time he hit a bump in the sand and the car flew a measured 30 feet before coming to a thumping slide, destroying another set of tires.

Campbell was beginning to show the strain of his many brushes with disaster. But he added a ton of lead ballast to the car to hold it down and brought it back to the starting line. Several more practice runs showed that it helped some, but even the slightest ripple in the sand caused wheelspin, and it was all the seasoned veteran could do to keep it from sliding broadside again.

The 1935 record run was the fastest "official" run ever made on the beach. Campbell had hit 330 miles per hour on one run, but trouble on the return dropped his average to 276.

Spectators lined the highway south of the grandstand, eagerly awaiting a run by Sir Malcolm Campbell.

Finally Campbell indicated that he was ready for another record attempt. Crew members, officials and spectators were silent and apprehensive as Campbell climbed into the cockpit. But a smile—although a weary one—and a wave eased the minds of all who watched. He fired the fierce Rolls engine and literally burned down the beach, with sand and salt spraying behind the car and blue flame trailing from the exhaust. There was no question that man had never traveled as fast as Campbell as he went through the traps. He had been clocked at an incredible speed of 330 miles per hour. But there was little jubilation among Campbell and the crew.

They knew, too well, that they must back it up with a run in the other direction within one hour to secure an *official* record. Campbell was one run away from officially becoming the first man over 300 miles per hour.

The tires were changed in plenty of time for the return and a pensive Campbell cleaned the salt spray from his own windshield. He climbed into the car, buckled his soft leather racing cap under his chin and lowered his goggles. The crew stepped away from the car and watched breathlessly as Campbell started the engine and prepared for the run.

Everything looked good until he hit a slight ripple in the sand. The car slid slightly to the left and just as he appeared to have it back under control and in a straight line once more, he hit another bump and the car spun sideways through the measured mile. It came safely to a stop, resting on shredded tires, but the return speed was far too slow for him to have averaged 300 miles per hour.

After several more runs—the best two of which gave him a new "official" record of 276.82 miles per hour—he elected to quit. Bitterly disappointed he left the beach, knowing full well that he would never again return to "his" course as a competitor.

Tuthill was there also for Campbell's 300 mile per hour run and describes it:

"Watching the Bluebird in that performance from a vantage point in the grandstand located in the Measured Mile was a weird experience. First, a black dot appeared far up the beach and quickly took shape as it approached in utter silence. The Bluebird was outrunning its exhaust noise. A blur and a sudden blast like a clap of thunder and it was gone."

"After the shock wave all heads turned. Now the car was out of sight in the other direction, obscured by a swirling sand. We did see a big blue ball of flame that hung in midair for a second and also disappeared. That ear-shattering blast and the eerie ball of flame when Campbell cut the throttle are the only memories I have as an eye-witness of the fastest run ever made on the world famous measured mile."

The most famous car ever to run on the beach, Sir Malcolm Campbell's Bluebird, was brought out again in the 70s for television cameras.

March 7, 1935, brought to a close a quarter-century of land speed record runs at Daytona Beach. It was the last world land speed record run on the sand.

But it was not over for Campbell. He moved his record attempt to the Bonneville Salt Flats at the invitation of Ab Jenkins. Early in September of 1935 they laid out a 13-mile course and marked it with a single black line of oil on the white surface. And on September 3, Campbell made a run of 305 miles per hour. On the return run an oil line cracked, spraying the windshield and filling the cockpit with fumes and smoke. Campbell was nearly unconscious as he came to a stop at the other end of the Salt Flats, but he had broken his record with an average speed of 301.13 miles per hour.

Campbell's major regret was that he was not able to set his final record on his beloved beach. Before his death on New Year's Eve 1949 he referred to Daytona Beach as his "second home."

"The real significance of the Campbell record runs and of the Bluebird and the Rolls-Royce engines was not apparent until a small fleet of Hurricane and Spitfire fighters reduced Hitler's mighty Luftwaffe to a shambles in the skies over London and prevented the invasion of Britain," says Tuthill.

"The reason those Spitfires and Hurricanes could fly continuously, day and night around the clock with little or no maintenance, was the speed, power, endurance and unbreakable qualities of the Rolls-Royce engines that powered them.

"The test bench for development of those remarkable engines was Sir Malcolm Campbell's Bluebird, and the proving ground was 17 miles of Daytona Beach straightaway. And that's why Leo Villa's crew had aircraft rather than automobile mechanics when they came to Daytona in 1933."

The Bluebird, together with the other Museum of Speed exhibits, will be enshrined in the new Motorsports Hall of Fame at Talladega, Alabama.

William H. G. France

Beach racing
Organization begins

William Henry Getty France was born in Washington, D.C., on September 26, 1909. It took him exactly 17 years to get around to building his first race car.

"Hugh Ostemeyer, a buddy of mine, and I built a race car out of the most inexpensive material any vehicle was ever made from." It was Bill France talking, the man who picked up the racing pieces on Daytona Beach after Sir Malcolm Campbell moved on; the man who was himself to achieve a sort of nobility in world racing circles. He relaxed his six-foot five, 220-pound frame in the recliner and looked out across the backyard of his spacious home on the banks of the Halifax River, half a mile from where it all started on Ormond Beach. And he spoke of the past.

"The car had a wooden body covered with canvas. It's a wonder it never caught fire and burned to the ground," he chuckled. "But it would run—eighty-five or ninety—with that old overhead valve Model T engine we built up."

It took France and Ostemeyer a couple of summers to get it ready, but by the time France was old enough to race, he had a ride. And he ran it on tracks around the District, mostly at a half-mile dirt track at Pikesville, Maryland.

"It was a good mechanical education, if nothing else," he says. "And I never got hurt, which is a miracle in itself, because I sure didn't know anything about strain on wheels or anything. But it was a start."

France had other interests; he played basketball at Central High School and worked parttime as a bank clerk and messenger at Commercial National Bank. But somehow his major efforts always got back to racing. He built a second race car after he graduated from high school, and he bought a motorcycle with earnings he had saved, so he divided racing interests between the car and the bike.

In 1927 he went to work for a Washington service station chain as a battery and electrical system repairman, then later to a local Ford dealer as a front-end specialist. He was picking up valuable knowledge to apply to his own machines. He was also watching how the cream of the racing crop drove the old Baltimore-Washington Speedway in Laurel, Maryland.

"It was a mile and an eighth board track and some of the best drivers in the country came there—men like Ralph DePalma and Harry Hartz—and I used to sit in the stands and study every move they made," he says.

He watched patiently until he got a chance to get on the track himself, which he did in his father's Model T.

"Dad didn't know it, of course," says France in his soft drawl. "The toughest part later was keeping a straight face when he went down to the tire dealer to complain about the tires wearing out so fast on the Model T."

France stepped up his racing activities by campaigning a Riley all over the Eastern circuit. He also stepped up his interest in Anne Bledsoe, a nurse whom he had met in D.C. one night at a dance at Children's Hospital. On June 23, 1931 France married Anne, who had come to Washington from Nathan's Creek, a tiny mountain community in North Carolina.

After the birth of their first son, William Clifton (Bill, Jr.) the Frances decided that the life of a mechanic-race driver would be better lived down South, so they bought a small house trailer, hooked it up to the Ford and headed south with all their belongings. It was 1934 and the destination was Miami.

"I had $25 in my pocket and another $75 in my bank account, and a set of old tools," says France. "And I figured that was all we needed to get a new start. If I was going to work on automobiles, I might just as well do it someplace where I wouldn't have to fight snow and cold weather."

They didn't get to Miami. When they reached Ormond Beach, the lure of that famous race course apparently was too much. Thoughts of Sir Malcolm Campbell and all the others drew him to the beach like a magnet.

"We drove across the Ormond Bridge and out on the beach," he says. "The tide was out and I remember looking down the beach and seeing that green water for the first time. It was a beautiful fall day, and there wasn't a soul on the beach.

"We drove on down the beach to the main pier at Daytona, and we changed into our bathing suits in the trailer and went swimming."

After spending a few days with friends in New Smyrna, the Frances came back to Daytona and rented a three-room bungalow for $13.50 a month. And then Bill got a job as a mechanic at the Daytona Motor Company, the local Pontiac, Buick and Cadillac dealer.

"A lot of newspaper and magazine stories over the years have said my car broke down, and that's why we settled in Daytona, but if that had happened, I could have fixed it. I just like Daytona, and we decided it was where we wanted to be," says France.

Between the races at dirt tracks all over the South and the ones he went back up North to run, France had built up a good reputation for himself by the time Malcolm Campbell made his final run on the beach. As France watched the Bluebird run, he felt very much a part of the Daytona racing scene. Following the run, he bought a service station so that he could devote more time to his own racing career.

"Business was not too good at first," France says, "so I had plenty of time to fish and race. Not bad."

It was a lucky break for the City of Daytona Beach. Bill France felt the lure of the famous shores that Campbell had felt, and, when the Englishman moved on, William H. G. France was there. It would take a few years, but little-by-little, step-by-step he would pick up the legacy Campbell had left behind. And more.

Millard Conklin—a Daytona attorney and sportsman—represented the city and was assisted by Sig Haughdahl in the planning and managing of the first Beach Road Race on the old 3.2 mile course.

Bill France was one of the early entries. France drove a '35 Ford V-8 coupe owned by a fellow mechanic named Glen Brooks. Ucal Cunningham—a Daytona gasoline distributor—sponsored France with fuel and tires for the event.

The city had put up some pretty big money at times to attract land speed racers—as much as $30,000 for some of the big runs like Kaye Don or Seagrave. But in 1936 the Depression was still too much of a reality for money to be readily available. Still they needed some major tourist attraction, and racing had to be it.

They went to Sig Haugdahl, the local garage owner, many time dirt track champion and the first man ever to run three miles a minute through the measured mile on the beach, and they asked his opinion. Sig had already discussed a beach-road race course with France, so together they outlined the concept that was not only unique but cheap to construct.

It turned out to be a course that would some day affect the future of auto and motorcycle racing in America, keep the city in the spotlight it had occupied since 1902 as speed capital of the world, and shape the future of Bill France.

The plan was ridiculed by many, but was finally adopted, simply because nobody else suggested anything better.

"The course went down the highway a mile and a half," says France, "made a turn in the sand and came back up the beach to the North Turn, just below the Measured Mile. With the narrow old black-top road, the two tight turns and the beach stretch, it was 3.2 miles around."

With the course built, they contacted the American Automobile Association, who had timed all of the speed runs on the beach, to sanction the 250-mile race. The purse was to be $5,000 for the "strictly stock automobile" race.

Because of the large-for-the-time purse, the race attracted many of the biggest names in the country. Among the entries were Indianapolis 500 winner Bill Cummings; dirt track champions Bob Sall, Doc MacKenzie and Ben Shaw; midget racing champion Bill Schindler; international racing star Major Goldie Gardner; the Collier brothers, Sam and Miles, two wealthy young sportsmen who later brought sports car racing to the front in America with races at Sebring and Watkins Glen, and Palm Beach millionaire Jack Rutherfurd, who was famous for his exploits in both cars and boats. And Bill France.

France entered a 1935 Ford and served as mechanic on another Ford driven by Milt Marion. Marion's car was one of the first to have sponsorship. Permatex had come up with some money for Marion and race officials allowed him to eliminate certain gaskets—ones like water pump and oil pan that had nothing to do with performance—so that he could use Parmatex gasket solution. Aside from Indianapolis, there wasn't any sponsorship in automobile racing in those days.

The cars were permitted to use any kind or size tires they wanted, but this didn't give them any particular advantage over the others because there *were* no special tires available. Most of the cars simply ran on the tires that had come on them.

National press coverage was extensive because of the quality of the field, attracting Bob Considine from the Associated Press, Henry McLemore, noted columnist, and reporters from many major newspapers and magazines. They all came to see the race on the unusual course. In fact, it captured the interest of the entire racing world.

Qualifying began long before the tide was all the way out to give them time to get in the 250 miles before it came back. Bill Cummings in a supercharged Auburn was the fastest qualifier with a 70.39 mile per hour average. But as the 27-car field qualified, there was also much action at City Hall. The project had become a political football and the race was in danger of being cancelled, even after the cars were on the beach. One faction had hidden the prize money and another has seized the tickets. So Haugdahl gathered together the most important newsmen he could find and they stormed City Hall. They got the money released.

"The tickets showed up later," said Haugdahl, "but only after several thousand people had gotten in free. But we really didn't care at that point. As long as we knew that we had the prize money, we were going to have a race."

Bill Schindler, the midget racing sensation of the East, was one of the favorites of the 1936 beach race. Here he sits in a midget featuring a basket of dry ice used to cool the tires.

Racing star Doc MacKenzie tries out the 1936 Buick pace car before the first beach race. The bevy of bathing beauties were unidentified.

Race cars line up for the start of the 1936 beach race.

The cars started in reverse order, with Cummings last and the slowest qualifier first. In an effort to give everybody an even chance, and to make the race more interesting for the fans, the cars were given handicaps also. The two slowest cars—both Willys'—made three laps before the next car was turned loose. Then cars were started at one or two minute intervals, depending on how fast they had qualified. Cummings started 30 minutes and 40 seconds after the first Willys.

"We didn't know until qualifying time if the beach was going to be rough or smooth," France says. "We knew that we'd have to wait until the tide was half-way out before we could tell if it was decent to run on. There was no other way. Then we had to worry about the wind, because if it changed, it could affect how far out the tide would go, and how fast it would come back in. We knew, for instance, that a strong east wind would bring a higher tide, so everybody constantly checked the wind and the beach."

Fortunately, the beach straightaway was smooth when the tide left. The field blasted off about one hour before it was all the way out.

Part of the huge crowd on hand for the 1936 race.

An unidentified driver peers over the wind-shield of his Ford in the deeply-rutted North Turn during the late stages of the 1936 race.

"I started tenth, about eight minutes after the first car, but it didn't take me long to pass both Willys'," says France. "Then, about 15 minutes after that, Bill Cummings came by me in the Auburn with the sand flying. I only saw him one more time in the race, and that was when he was in the pits," he recalls.

Cummings didn't last long. The Auburn was low and the sand apparently was scooped up under the hood and sucked into the supercharger. It took only 16 laps to destroy the mighty engine. Rutherfurd, in the other Auburn, lasted 26 laps.

The incoming tide catches one of the racers on the last lap of the 1936 beach course race.

Milt Marion, the eventual winner of the first beach course race in 1936, slides through the South Turn.

Milt Marion, winner of the first beach race. He was also one of the first cars to have sponsorship.

Eight miles of cars make a hasty exit after the 1936 race, trying to avoid the incoming tide.

Indianapolis 500 winner Wild Bill Cummings was the favorite in the first beach course race, but his supercharged Auburn lasted only 16 laps, because of sand in the blower.

"The big, heavy cars had a disadvantage," says France. "Cummings and Rutherfurd in the Auburns and Gardner in the Lincoln Zephyr just didn't last, so it wasn't too many laps before we all felt it would be a Ford at the finish.

"I had an advantage over a lot of them, because I had been there for a couple of years and I knew how to drive in the sand. If you're interested in racing at all, you just don't live at the beach without using it."

Many of the race cars got in trouble late in the race because the turns had rutted out so much. Most of them got stuck at one time or another. If they went too slow, they mired down and had to be towed out. If they went too fast, they dug in and flipped, so it became a delicate trick to find just the right speed. A mile or two either way resulted in disaster of one sort or another.

Milt Marion was towed out five times, but, after each incident, he drove like mad and caught whomever he thought was the leader. And that, in itself, was no easy task to figure out. Race officials themselves weren't even too sure who was leading.

As if the confusion of the rutted course and tow trucks everywhere wasn't enough, the east wind did come up and the tide started back in much sooner than had been expected. There became a chance that hundreds of spectators' cars would be stranded on the beach after the race. So, when there was a tangle in the North Turn that completely blocked the course at about the 200-mile mark, the race was called and Milt Marion was declared the winner—in the France-prepared Ford.

"How they figured out who won the race, I don't know," says France. "They said Marion won, Ben Shaw was second and Tommy Elmore was third, but nobody really knew. There was so much confusion. Marion may have won. They said I finished fifth, but I may have been tenth. Or I may have won.

"Kenny Schroeder of Jamestown, New York, came up to me after the race and asked 'You got any idea who won? Or where I finished?' And I couldn't tell him because I didn't even know where *I* had finished."

As rocky—or sandy—as the beginning was, it was even rougher for the city. They announced that they had lost a whopping $22,000 on the event, and, as far as they were concerned, it was the end of the line for beach racing at Daytona.

The city may have given up, but not everybody else. Men like France and Haugdahl were not so easily discouraged. They contacted the local Elks Club and talked them into backing a stock car race for 1937. And then they went back to the beach to study why it hadn't actually worked. They knew that they had to overcome the rutting problem, otherwise it would be another tow truck race.

There is a clay in the Daytona area called "marl," that turns to a sort of powered limestone when it dries, and they found that if they added that to the turns, it stabilized them. So they got huge stockpiles of the clay and announced that they had solved the problem of the 1936 race. They also announced that the 1937 race would be held on Labor Day.

It was all speculation, because they couldn't really do anything to the course in advance of race day. The tides would undo anything they improved. They simply had to wait until the last tide went out before the race and then rush in with the equipment to add the marl to the turns, knowing full well that it would last but one low tide.

The minute the tide started out, they frantically went to work, adding clay to the turns, smoothing it out with a road grader, and then going over it many times with a steam roller, trying to match as well as possible the joint between their own work and mother nature's.

"It wasn't easy to do," says France, "because we didn't know from one tide to the next what the beach was going to be like, and we didn't know how much we were going to have to do to the straightaway. The tides would either raise or lower the beach, and this created a problem with our work on the turns. Even the direction of the wind had an effect. If you got a west wind, the tide would *roughen* the beach, and if you got a sustained northeast wind, it would *smooth* the beach. It was never the same two days in a row.

The Volusia County road crews worked quickly, and the cars got qualified about the time the tide was all the way out.

The race itself had been scheduled for only 50 miles because they were not sure how their course improvements were going to work over a longer haul.

"The turns dug up some at the point where the clay and the sand met," says France, "but it was a definite improvement over the year before, and it gave us some idea where to go from there."

Smokey Purser, a local bar owner, won that 50-miler with Mike Cone coming in second. Both of them were in Fords. Purser won $43.56.

Nineteen-thirty-eight was the year that Bill France began his career as a race promoter. The Elks Club followed the city's path and retired from sponsoring the event, so France and restaurant owner Charlie Reese picked up the reins, promoting it themselves.

A 25 cent phone call, however, was to be the determining factor in pushing France into the promoting business. Ralph Hankinson was a well-known race promoter, having held events at places like Langhorne, Pennsylvania, and other eastern tracks. He lived close to Daytona in Orange City Beach, so he was the first person France thought about when the Elks Club pulled out.

"I didn't have the quarter for the long distance phone call," says France, "so I called him collect. Well, he wouldn't accept the charges, so I just decided to promote it myself. That's when I called Charlie Reese. It wasn't a toll call.

"Charlie and I charged 50 cents for admission," says France, "and 5,000 people showed up. We divided $200 profit when it was all over. The next race we upped the price to one dollar, and just as many people came, so we split $2,200. I had never seen that much money at one time. And it taught me a lesson: we had undersold the product the first time out. I never forgot that lesson."

Right from the beginning, France tried to bring some order to racing. And some integrity.

"I always felt I could improve on the job a lot of promoters were doing," he says. "Not all of them were honest. For example, the one in Pikesville, where I used to race when I was a kid, announced one night on the P.A. that we should get our cars to the line because this was a big race, paying $500 to win. Well, when I finished third and got ten dollars, I went up and asked if there was that much difference in the payoff between first and third. 'Oh, that was just for the benefit of the public. We only paid the winner $50,' they told me. I always remembered that."

Another factor France tried to eliminate from racing was cheating.

"We got specifications from the auto manufacturers, so that we had something to match when we had the inspection after the race, but they (the manufacturers) kept changing things and we had a hard time keeping up with what was stock and what wasn't. The inspections after the race always took more time than the race itself. They were held at the City Yard Garage and usually lasted all night. I mean, they tore down engines and every part was checked."

The 1938 Labor Day race was considerably more organized. For one thing, it was the first time a public address system had been used in beach races, and, for the first time, spectators had some idea what was going on out there. The entire race was more interesting, mainly because they had

Bill France campaigned the Blitzkreig Special all over the South before World War II.

further perfected the method for stabilizing the turns. They didn't dig up until the last few laps of the race.

Smokey Purser again led the way and was well out in front at the end of the 160-mile race. In fact, when the checkered flag dropped, Smokey kept right on going, up the beach and out of sight. It left the entire crowd bewildered. Everybody, that is, but Ed Parkinson, who was head of the technical committee.

"We knew Smokey must have something on that car he didn't want checked right then," Parkinson said, "why else would he not come back to get the trophy? So I got a couple of guys and we went looking for him."

They found Purser in Roy Strange's Garage. And, as you might guess, Purser and Strange were frantically trying to put the engine back to its stock configuration. They had found that Ford built some special high compression heads for cars they sold in the Denver area, heads to compensate for the higher altitude. Purser had gotten his hands on a set of the "Denver heads," but he had to get them off before the post-race inspection. He was disqualified on the spot, and second place finisher Bill France was declared the winner.

"They credited me with winning," says France, "but my partner Charlie Reese said, 'lissen, we can't give you the first place money. I mean, you being one of the promoters and all, so let's give the money to the *third place car*'."

And that's how the 1938 race ended. Smokey Purser won it but didn't get credit for the victory; Bill France got official credit for the win but didn't get the money, and Lloyd Moody got the money but didn't get credit for winning.

There were two races in 1939 with no controversial finishes in either one. The speed and the quality of the racing was going up. In the first race, the cars hit more than 100 miles per hour on the road section, and the lead changed hands several times between Joe Littlejohn, France and Sam Rice.

France took the lead on the 32nd lap, and it looked as if he had the race won. He began to stretch the lead, but he was forced to pit for fuel. He was out of the pits in an amazing 11 seconds, but, as it turned out, the pit stop was *too* quick. His pick-up pit crew had not gotten in enough fuel and he had to pit again a few laps later. Littlejohn took the lead at that point but flipped his car in the South Turn on the following lap. He got back in the race, but it was too late. Rice had built up too much of a lead in his '39 Mercury. Rice averaged 70.34 miles per hour in winning. Littlejohn managed to finish second, Stuart Joyce was third, Purser was fourth and Lloyd Moody was fifth.

The second race that year was even more exciting. A slough on the beach section bounced the cars around and produced a water spray that blinded the drivers behind the lead cars. They swerved all over the beach and the crowd got its money's worth. France led the first lap but Joyce took over on the next one with his Mercury-powered Ford. He led until Lap 28, when he flipped going into the South Turn. For the next few laps, it was a battle between France and Purser, but Joyce, who hadn't lost all that much time in the crash, caught them and took the lead on Lap 33. They couldn't catch him. Joyce won with a record average of 76.03 mph. He won $350 for first place and another $232 in lap prizes. Purser was second, Bill Turner third, France fourth and Bill Snowden fifth.

The following day, the *Daytona Beach Morning Journal* echoed the feeling of many fans about one of their hometown heroes:

> Purser went down in racing annals as being about the best driver in the turns ever to sit behind a wheel. The veteran local driver hit the turn at its outer edge and skidded on a long curve into the rise, then eased over into the road, without losing any speed, it seemed.

Beach racing was growing up.

In 1940, Joe Littlejohn came within two-tenths of a second of breaking the 80 mile per hour barrier in qualifying his Buick. That was just the beginning of the excitement for the 10,000 spectators. The race was to be a dogfight from start to finish, with a couple of hotshots from Atlanta, Bob Flock and 19-year-old Roy Hall, challenging the Daytona veterans, France and Purser, and Spartanburg's Littlejohn. Each of them had a turn out front.

As the race wore on, it was Hall, whose outstanding handling in the corners finally outclassed Littlejohn's straightaway speeds. The Atlantan took the lead on Lap 29 and was never headed. Behind him cars were flipping into the dunes with great regularity. Larry Grant flipped early in the race, and the resulting crash was so spectacular that they forced him into an ambulance, but he escaped and jumped back into his Willys, finishing the race in 15th place.

The talk of the day, however, was Hall's pit stop action. *The Daytona Beach Evening News* reported:

> *There was some discussion among fans and announcers that Hall didn't stop for gas. Other pit men said the gang of workmen that handled Roy's car looked like a group of trained monkeys when Hall stopped. They literally ate him up with service. In fact, the time on his stop was 40 seconds—no wonder no one missed him in the race.*

There was little mention of Flock or of his mechanic, Red Vogt, but the racing world was to hear much more from them.

The July 4 race in 1940 was a decisive victory for France. He led the entire race in his Buick, followed by Littlejohn in another Buick and Purser and Bill Snowden in Fords.

George Ruse drove a Chevy pick-up in the race and crashed when an elderly couple, crossing the course, fell down in front of his race truck.

Another see-saw battle took place in the first 1941 race. The lead changed hands between France, Lloyd Seay, Bill Snowden, Purser and Roy Hall in the "Bundles for Britain" charity race.

Rough sand caused many crashes, notably 1938 Stock Car Champion Lloyd Seay, who flipped on three different occasions.

A second Flock brother, Fontello (who would rise to fame as "Fonty") appeared on the scene, as did another southern hero, Jap Brogden. But it was Hall who put his Ford in the lead on the 42nd lap and kept it there to win. Purser was second, Tommy Elmore third and Stuart Joyce fourth. *The Daytona Beach Evening News*, in listing the prizes, reported: "Marvel Gallentyne of New Smyrna Beach was 16th finisher and won three pairs of socks."

Twelve thousand fans saw the Frank Lockhart Memorial Race, which was the last event before World War II temporarily halted beach activity. Held only four weeks after the first 1941 race, it was France on the pole with a supercharged Graham. He led the first 20 laps, but was forced out of the race with engine trouble. Purser took over and led until Lap 33, when he was forced to pit. Roy Hall, who had started last in the 42-car field, was ninth after five laps. Hall charged into the lead, but was unable to hold off Purser in the last lap. The Daytona driver thrilled the partisan crowd as he passed Hall on the beach straight to win.

Harry (Three Wheeler) Sheeler provided much of the drama by flipping his car once on its nose, once on its top and another time on its side. He was running at the finish.

The war ended the second era of beach racing.

Racing took another turn after the war, as promoters used every gimmick in the book to appeal to the entertainment-starved masses. They created championship titles for almost everyone as they tried to pick up the tempo that had been stilled by the war clouds. At any given stock car race in the South, there might be competition between the National Stock Car Champion, the World Stock Car Champion, the Dirt Track Champion, and simply the National Champion, the Southern Champion and the Georgia and Florida Champions.

But, call them what they wanted, most came from Atlanta. And it didn't help all that much. The races were highly unorganized. It was a big blast for one day and then they all went home and made moonshine and raced around the back roads. Then they raced somewhere else the next weekend.

Bill Tuthill, who came to Daytona after World War II, remembers the period:

"In the scheme of things, it didn't mean much," he said. "They were mostly a bunch of numbers guys and bootleggers, and most of the money involved was passed back and forth between *them*. There weren't big purses, but there were big wagers. I've seen many fellows betting a thousand dollars on a race where the official winner's purse was $50.

"They were pretty desperate characters, most of them," Tuthill continued. "They were outrunning cops and being shot at and all of those things. But, you know, they were polite and soft-spoken. They were really a wonderful bunch of guys to be around."

Bill France had spent the war years building submarine chasers. Following the war, he opened a lounge on top of the Streamline Hotel. It was here that all the racers gathered to drink and live it up, telling stories of their latest techniques for evading the law. The sessions lasted until the wee small hours.

"Anybody that came up with a crude idea like, say, throwing a glass jug out of the window into the path of the car chasing him was considered an amatuer," says Tuthill. "This was considered 'kid stuff' by these guys. They had far more sophisticated methods; like rigging up a pump that would inject a fluid into the exhaust and set up a smoke screen. That might be the hot set-up for one time, but the next time they got together maybe somebody had come up with a solution that would not only smoke like mad, but would leave an oil film on the windshield of the guy chasing him.

"Those were the kind of things that brought a pat on the back to the guy who invented them," he says. "But they could drive. I mean, they drove on back roads at night with their lights off, and they flew. Why, they could spin a car 180 degrees in its own length without backing off."

Tuthill, of course was speaking of the "bootleg turn," which was something they used to evade a pursuer. It gave them some sort of "status" in the South. The bootleg turn was no small accomplishment.

"Those were the racers of the day," says Tuthill. "Some of them you never heard about again." He paused, running a hand through his snow white hair. "They probably went to jail. It wasn't all that uncommon.

"Why, at Lakewood in Atlanta, they had a ban on anybody racing that had ever been arrested," he says. "That made for some pretty funny episodes. Once the cops tried to stop the races and the fans ran off the cops. It might seem like this didn't have too much to do with Daytona, except that it was mostly these same guys that came down here to race. It was the same guys who were racing all over the South.

"They wouldn't let Bob Flock race at Lakewood because he had been arrested for hauling moonshine, so one night he waited until the race had already started and he just came onto the track in the back straightaway. Well, when the cops found out that he was in the race, they started chasing him. On the track. It was like an episode of the Keystone Cops: the race cars came sliding around that old dirt track, pushing and bumping, with dust flying, and here came the cops, right in the middle of the action.

"After several laps, Bob gave the 'hi' sign to his buddies in the pits," Tuthill continued, "and the next time around, Bob came right down through the pits and right out the back gate the guys had opened for him. He went right out onto the street with the cops hot in pursuit. Right through downtown Atlanta. He finally gave himself up, because he was running out of gas. 'Well, hell, what did I do wrong?' he asked, as he got out of his race car."

Flock was not the only one who became the target of the law because of his illegal whiskey endeavors, Tuthill recalls.

"There were a couple of guys down here that got caught for making and selling peach brandy. I can't even remember their names, but I remember the incident. The cops had arrested them and had confiscated their car. Well, these guys got out on bail, and they simply broke into the compound area behind the police station, stole their own car and raced it that weekend.

"You know, though, it was just like I said: they were nice guys to talk to. They also had their own code. Call it the 'Law of the West,' call it what you want, but they had an honor about them. Like Buddy Shuman, who was one of the first really great drivers to become well-known after the war. Well, Buddy was from Charlotte—and somewhat of a rival for the Atlanta gang—and he had also been known to run a little whiskey from time to time.

"Buddy was out driving one day on the back roads around Charlotte," says Tuthill, "and a deputy sheriff started chasing him, I guess, just because he recognized Buddy.

"Buddy took off—not because he had any whiskey, he didn't, but, would you believe it, because he didn't have his driver's license with him and he didn't want to get a ticket for that. So he gave the sheriff a real run for his money, until he came to a washed out bridge. That was definitely the end of the chase," Tuthill chuckles. But there is a definite look of respect in his eyes as his mind races back to the "good old days."

"That deputy was shaking like a leaf when he got out of his car, and Buddy smiled a great big smile at him. But the deputy pulled a pistol and stuck it right up to Buddy's throat. And he pulled the trigger. Nobody could ever explain it, but the bullet didn't hit any arteries or anything. Buddy carried that scar for the rest of his life.

"Well, they put Buddy on a chain gang, and he served the time. He could have gotten off because he had a lot of influential friends around, but he didn't want anything to do with probation. He wanted to serve his time and be completely free when he got out. He was determined to do it right.

"This is the type of guys you were dealing with," Tuthill says. "Oh, there may have been a few real desperados, but they were few and far between. Most of them were guys like Buddy and Bob.

"A lot of these guys, however, contributed nothing to racing but their presence," he says. "But it wasn't too long after the war that racing started to assume a purpose. It got to be that it was no longer just a bunch of guys 'getting together.'

"Roy Hall and the Flock brothers and Shuman and Marshall Teague and some of the guys of that era were fantastic drivers. You can't downgrade them a bit just because there still wasn't a whole lot of organization. As for driving skill, they had it. On or off the track.

"Those early races were heart-stoppers," says Tuthill. "Nobody would give an inch, and if you didn't get out of the way, they'd run over you. When the flag dropped you'd think war was declared. They went anyplace there was an opening—down through the pits, in the grass, the infield, anywhere."

In 1946 beach racing started again. It was a classic example of that wild and woolly style of stock car racing, bringing together a lot of the stars from the pre-war years with some of the new ones. Daytona was on the racing map again.

The nation needed the wildness of stock car racing. The seriousness of war had passed and the South, in particular, was looking again for heroes to worship. Red Byron was perfect for the role. He was a wounded war veteran, a tail gunner whose leg had been so badly mangled by Japanese flack that he had to wear a steel brace. His mechanic had to design a special clutch for him. In fact, his left shoe was actually bolted to the clutch.

To make things more dramatic, his mechanic was also a redhead from Atlanta, and was to become one of the best-known "wrenches" in the business—Red Vogt.

The race pitted Byron and Roy Hall, one of the heroes of pre-war days. The two Atlantans battled furiously, with Hall taking an early lead, only to lose it when he slid into the ocean. Byron roared into the lead, but hit a fence on the 17th lap. Hall took over again but lost a wheel and crashed at the half-way point. Byron was in front to stay, finishing two miles ahead of Joe Littlejohn, Ed Eng and Bill France. France was now the sole promoter of the event.

It had been a long time coming, but Bill France had brought stock car racing to the front, becoming a full-time promoter along the way.

The 1947 race started off faster than any one ever had. As engine failure gnawed away at the early leaders, it became more and more apparent that the cool driving ability of Byron and the durability of Vogt cars would pay off.

Ed Samples of Atlanta opened the race with a pace of more than 93 miles per hour. He had lapped one car at the end of only five laps when his engine let go. Jack Ethridge, also of Atlanta, took the lead and built up a three mile advantage over second place driver Bob Flock, but Ethridge's car also was unable to survive the strenuous pace.

Here is how the *Illustrated Speedway News* summed up the race:

> *One by one, the early leaders fell by the wayside and the steady driving Byron kept on plugging away to cash in on a nice job of driving, endurance and mechanical efficiency. Byron was tailing Ethridge and (Bill) Snowden at the 10th lap mark. He had advanced to the runner-up spot at 20 laps. He surged in front on the 21st lap and dueled (Marshall) Teague almost neck and neck to the 30th lap. Motor trouble spoiled Teague's chances in the 34th lap, and Flock jumped into the No. 2 position.*
>
> *At the end of 40 laps, Byron was ahead by a handsome margin and Flock was second. They raced in that order until Flock threw his wheel (into the crowd, injuring two spectators) in the 45th lap, setting the stage for (Louis) Puckett to go into second spot. Puckett had careened into a ditch at the north turn earlier in the race, but he pulled out.*
>
> *At the finish Byron was too far in front for competition and the fans were not in doubt about the final outcome.*
>
> *Byron had things pretty much his own way in the home stretch, what with the number of fastest cars on the blink, and he did not have to bang 'er to the floorboard in the waning laps.*

The motorcycles, which had been running on the beach since 1937, still drew larger crowds than the modifieds. The Daytona 200 motorcycle classic for 1947 drew a field of 184 riders from nearly every state in the Union and most of the Canadian provinces. It also attracted the largest crowd in the history of the beach, encouraging France to bring back the modifieds in July of 1947. Again it proved to be a success as race cars showed up from all over the South.

Red Vogt brought two cars this time, with Byron and Bob Flock to do the driving duties. Ed Samples, Gober Sosebee and Fonty Flock, also from

Atlanta, Buddy Shuman of Charlotte, and local hero Marshall Teague gave the crowd a spectacular show.

With all the big names, it was easy to overlook a tall, skinny teenager who had served his apprenticeship in Teague's workshop. The newcomer quietly stood beside his own race car and watched in silent respect as *his* heroes qualified. Glenn "Fireball" Roberts began his beach-racing career, one that would establish him as one of the greatest stock car drivers of all time. The nickname "Fireball" had been given him because of his ability as a baseball player, although few would remember that.

Daytona sports editor Benny Kahn wound up his story of that 1947 race with this comment:

> *Roberts' showing in his first outing here won him praise along Gasoline Alley. The reckless Daytonan creased the curves at breakneck speed and gave the thrill-seeking audience a run for its money.*

It was a phrase that was to follow him for the rest of his relatively short life: "He gave the audience a run for its money."

More than 10,000 fans showed up for the race, giving France the incentive and the money to improve the course, something that he had considered for a long time. A study of the situation convinced him that the only thing to do was move the whole course farther south on the beach.

"It was getting so built up near the course at Wilbur that we decided to move down the peninsula as far as we could go," says France. "I guess even then we could see the handwriting on the wall, so I figured that the farther south we went, the longer we could race on the beach."

It was the kind of forethought that would mark Bill France's promotional career from that point on. He had already learned to be a traffic control expert of sorts.

"You have no idea," says Bill Tuthill, "how bad traffic got after those beach races, but Bill knew when to start them and when to end them, and where to park the spectator's cars."

France was able to select Speed Week dates and handle traffic and parking with such success that thousands of autos were moved away from the course after a race with only a few being stuck in the sand, or even worse, in the surf. He was described, too, as being a "one-man counterpart of the *Farmer's Almanac*." He won fame for his long-range ability to figure out the best times to race on the beach—winds and the Atlantic Ocean notwithstanding. And all this time he was building more and more interest in stock car racing. The sport was gaining in popularity at an astonishing rate—unmatched, perhaps, by any other.

The initial beach course had been 3.2 miles in length. The new one was to be 4.1 miles for bikes and 2.2 miles for cars. To accomplish this, France designed a turn-off halfway up the straightaway to be used by the cars. They were to slide in there and complete the circuit on the short course. New "permanent" bleachers were built.

"They were permanent only in the vaguest sense of the word," says France, "because, like the others, a good, strong wind could come up and blow them down."

The course was readied for the 1948 beach race.

1947-1958
NASCAR 4
Order from chaos
End of beach racing

"We started getting a number of requests from other track operators to help them run their races," France recalls. "I ran one with Bill Tuthill at Lonsdale, Rhode Island. It was on a one-third mile asphalt track and was probably the first time stocks had ever run on anything bigger than a half-mile.

"I organized eight or ten races in '47, under the name of National Championship Stock Car Circuit. It was run right from my home with Anne handling the point fund that we'd developed for the races at Greenville-Pickens, Greensboro, Spartanburg, North Wilkesboro, Rhode Island and the beach. Anne has been an active partner in all our races since World War II.

"We ended the season in Jacksonville, dividing a point fund worth about $3,000, and I could see how much interest there was. In fact, there had been a lot of interest up north, too, so after the Jacksonville race, I called a number of people from both north and south and asked them to come to Daytona to see if we could expand our little group into a bigger racing association."

France and Tuthill had formed a solid friendship that was to have a profound bearing on auto racing from then on.

It was that Fall that a group got together at the roof garden of the Streamline Hotel in Daytona Beach to talk about forming a stronger organization. At 1 p.m. on December 14, 1947—a Sunday—Bill France called to order the First Annual Convention of the National Championship Stock Car Circuit. The minutes show the following present:

Freddy Horton, Providence; Joe Ross, Boston; Jack Higgins and Tom Lovarco, Ft. Lauderdale; Tom Galan, Harvey Tattersall and Fred Dagvar, New York; Ed Bruce and Jack Peters, Berea, Ohio; Jimmy Cox, Mt. Airy, N.C.; Chick DiNatale and Bill Streeter, Trenton; Fred Zimmerman, Ft. Lauderdale; Bill Tuthill, Jimmy Roberts, Bill Kleeby, Bernard Kahn, Lucky Sauer and Bob Barry, Daytona; Jimmy Quisenberry, Washington, D.C.; Larry Roller, International News Service; Eddie Bland, Jacksonville; Alvin Hawkins and Joe Littlejohn, Spartanburg, and Buddy Shuman, Charlotte. Arriving Monday were: Bob Osieki, Bob Richards, Ed Samples and Red Vogt, Atlanta, and Marshall Teague, Daytona. Frank Munday, Tommy Garback and Sammy Packard arrived Tuesday.

The first official remarks of the meeting were made by France, who was introduced simply as "Director." He had appointed Bill Tuthill as temporary chairman of the four-day meeting.

It was a simple beginning to the annual meeting of the National Championship Stock Car Circuit, but what was to happen in the action-filled convention would have a lasting effect on stock car racing—and world-wide racing, for that matter—for all time.

France's opening remarks were built around his personal goal, a national stock car association with some power. He said:

> Nothing stands still in the world. Things get better or worse, bigger or smaller.
>
> Stock car racing has been my whole life. I've gone to other territories; I've left home, and I've always tried to develop something as I was going. I've tried to build up instead of tearing down.
>
> The first (strictly) stock car racing that I became associated with was here in 1936....After the old speed trails on the beach were taken away, Daytona was looking for something else to take their place, so they came up with a strictly stock car race, and they lost $22,000, so they pulled out....
>
> An average man in a fast automobile can still win races. It's just like Ted Horn in his Indianapolis racer against a boy in a cheap Ford. Horn could run off and hide from him, because the average boy doesn't have the money to improve his equipment....
>
> A dirt track is more than necessary to make a stock car race a good show. In fact, stock car races not held on dirt are nowhere near as impressive. To look their best, stock cars need dirt. Or sand. Oh, I was associated with Bill Tuthill at Lonsdale, Rhode Island, and it was pretty good on asphalt. It was almost dark when the race was over, and if the boys would have put on an extra lap or two, we could have seen how the lights worked for stock cars. But nobody left. I guess it proved that even on asphalt, nobody wanted their money back.
>
> We have to think about the image. If you get a junky old automobile, it's a jalopy in the average person's mind. Even if you take a new Cadillac and pull the fenders off and let it get real dirty, it would be a jalopy to most people.

This meeting in the smoke filled room atop the Streamline Hotel gave NASCAR its birth in 1947. Seated at the head table for this historic meeting were, from left, Joe Littlejohn, Bill Tuthill and Bill France.

Red Vogt was the first mechanical superstar of NASCAR *racing. His Atlanta garage turned out some of the fastest cars in racing history. In addition to supplying cars and top drivers, he gave* NASCAR *its name.*

Stock car racing has got distinct possibilities for Sunday shows. It would allow race-minded boys that work all week, who don't have the money to afford a regular racing car, to be competitive with a rich guy. It would allow them the opportunity to go to a race track on Sunday and to show their stuff, and maybe win a prize, and not make it their full-time job. We don't know how big it can be, I doubt if anybody here knows that, but I do know that if stock car racing is handled properly, it can go the same way big car racing has gone. Or bicycle racing, or any racing.

And if you have an event where you can publicize talent, then there is much better cooperation from the newspaper.

There are a whole lot of things to be straightened out here. We've got to get track owners and promoters interested in building up stock car racing. I would like to get all of us in accord on as many different subjects as we can bring up. Tomorrow morning I would like to appoint some committees for laying down rules and regulations which can be followed by the majority of the promoters and drivers. That will keep the whole thing on more or less a fair basis. . . .

Stock car racing as we've been running it is not, in my opinion, the answer. If it were, I wouldn't worry about anybody else. I would like to see to it that the average American boy, say, in Miami, if he runs according to the rules, is going to be able to run if he goes to Ft. Lauderdale or Atlanta or even Trenton. . . .

The main purpose of the technical committee will be to get a uniform automobile over the circuit. I believe stock car racing can become a nationally recognized sport by having a national point standing which will embrace the majority of large stock car events. . . . Regardless of whether you win a race in New England or Florida, the points would apply in the national championship bracket. What it would amount to is we'd have a national champion who had won his spurs on a national championship basis. . . .

And we should have a national benevolent fund . . . that protects boys who are laid up. There are things that come up from time to time, like the mechanic who gets hurt working on a car or the new driver who makes up his mind the day before the race to compete. They don't have time to get insurance, so we should be able to protect them. . . .

This touches just about everything I had in mind. Right here within our group rests the outcome of stock car racing in the country today. We have the opportunity to set it up on a big scale. I don't mean we can convert all of the men in the association, they have their own minds, but if the picture is bright enough and the boys have some goal in mind, or at the end of the year, when this thing is over, they've got some national recognition or a little money out of a point fund, and if everybody puts on races according to rules, and contributes money to the point fund, then it will mean something, and the boys in Ohio will want to have their own cars fixed up where they can come over and compete . . . We are all interested in one thing: Improving present conditions.

France must have fired the group to some action because he immediately appointed technical and competition committees. And then they voted to elect France president of the governing body. Also on the board were Bland and Tuthill as promoters, Osiecki and Dagavar as owners, Byron and Shuman as drivers, Teague and Vogt as mechanics and Bruce and Peters as roadster advisors. Samples was elected chairman of the technical committee and Dagavar chairman of the competition committee.

The next major order of business was the selection of a name for the new organization. Red Byron quickly moved to adopt National Stock Car Racing Association (NSCRA) as the name. It was seconded by Buddy Shuman and voted on. But, following recess for lunch, Red Vogt suggested that National

Association for Stock Car Auto Racing would be a better name for the organization. He asked for another vote. NSCRA received seven votes, NASCAR got four, mainly because somebody had pointed out that NASCAR sounded too much like Nash-Car.

Then somebody pointed out that there already was an association in Georgia with the NSCRA name, so Ed Bruce moved that the voting for the name on the previous ballot be disregarded and that they start from scratch, incorporating in Florida under the name of National Association for Stock Car Auto Racing. Jack Peters seconded, and it became the official name of the new organization.

Before adjournment of the four-day meeting, France appointed Cannonball Baker as high commissioner of the association.

Louis Ossinsky, Sr., a local attorney, assisted with the incorporation. France looked for a headquarters building, which he found at 800 Main Street—the second floor of a building that had once been a bank. The business cards would read well: NASCAR, Selden Bank Building, 800 Main Street, Daytona Beach, Florida.

In reality it was a crowded, $40-a-month walkup cubby hole with a creaky wooden stairway, but it was the spawning ground of what was to become the world's largest racing organization.

"The reason everything had gone so smoothly is that it had all been planned," says Tuthill. "We had made a study of every racing organization that had ever come along, so I told Bill that the democratic method, where the board voted on everything, had never worked.

"Just about the time the thing gets rolling," he told France, "there is some dissidence; somebody gets irked and they vote the guy out of office that had done all the spadework. So we went to the lawyer and told him to set up the organization as a private corporation.

"Bill didn't think it would work," says Tuthill, "but I said 'let's try it.' That's why he had appointed me as chairman of the meeting, and I, in turn, nominated him as president of the new association.

"That first meeting included some of the guys from rival groups," Tuthill says. "And we knew they were just there to see what we were going to do. They never would have come with us. There was no way we could ever bring this entire group together.

"Well, one fellow kept saying we should have a set of by-laws," he says, "but that's the last thing in the world we wanted. We were going to make our own by-laws, so we kept saying 'it's going to be taken care of.'

"We put a bunch of guys on committees, you know, 'you're the rules committee, and you're the specifications committee. Go off and meet.' But it was a ruse to get some of the guys out of our hair. I told Bill, 'You know they're going to get over there and get to arguing about quick-change rearends or gear ratios or whatever, so they meet all day and nothing happens and it gives us a breather for another year'."

NASCAR's slogan, right from the start, was "racing that is open to everybody." And it didn't take long to catch on.

"We were getting cars everywhere," says France, "like the Buffalo Civic Stadium. We had 275 cars in that area. And by getting this mass basis, we were able to get insurance where we might not have been able to otherwise. The insurance company wasn't interested in one race in DeLand and one over there. We gave them a whole schedule of races."

NASCAR got started on good footing. They appointed a chief steward at each race, so instead of going through all of the usual paperwork if there was a claim, he simply served as the claims adjuster.

"Since we had our own man at the track," says Tuthill, "and since he wasn't elected but appointed, it was simple. If he didn't do the job we *dis*appointed him. You know, a lot of times when I look back at it, I think we had more nerve than brains. We guaranteed the insurance company we would run 300 races the next year. At $100 each for the coverage, it came to $30,000. So we had to go out and get them going. And do you know, we had 394 that second year. We went from 85 to 394 races. In one year."

"We were on our way," says France. "We had real insurance—legitimate insurance—and I guess we were partly in the insurance business, too, because we processed the claims, notified the hospital to send us the bills, and we paid them immediately.

"The deal we had with the insurance company was a reimbursment one. We could send the check the next day and then submit the claim to the company," he said. "It was good because, in most cases, race drivers had ended up as charity cases unless they could pay their own bills."

"NASCAR was the first racing organization with real insurance," says Tuthill. "The others had a sort of benevolent fund and was subject to the whims of the organization. But, suddenly, here was a racing organization that paid hospital bills. Doctors were being paid and it gave NASCAR a tremendous amount of stature."

"It was something we were proud of," says France. "And the insurance company had to have a lot of faith in us, too. We added our own touches, like insuring all our own personnel—chief stewards, promoters, everybody. It also protected us from lawsuits."

"I think the reason everybody accepted NASCAR right from the beginning," says Tuthill, "was because Bill and all of us made an honest effort not to line our own pockets. 'If you come up with something good, the money should come along with it' was always a sort of personal motto with us. It was the premise on which NASCAR was founded.

"Our point fund was administered with honesty and integrity, too. If someone had had sticky fingers, he could easily have skimmed off the cream. I know it was Bill France's nature, and it was mine, to keep it completely honest.

"One of the biggest thrills all of us had was at the Victory Dinner the second year," Tuthill continues. "We had $64,000 in the point fund in the bank. We wanted to drop a bombshell at that dinner by actually giving it to the drivers right there. It was spread down to regional and state levels, and word went out that everybody had to come to the dinner to get their check. If they had $100 waiting, they had to come to Daytona to get it. Of course, it killed two birds with one stone: it impressed them to no end, and they usually *raced* while they were there. We got some good drivers from a long way off.

"We got a little paranoid with all that money in the bank," he recalls. "We were afraid that somebody might come up with a gripe and legally tie it all up, so we took it all out by writing the checks to the guys well in advance. And what a thrill it was at the banquet. I was M.C. and I got up and said, 'Okay, you guys, this is the point fund you've all heard about,' and I held up the stack of checks.

"I told them, 'I don't care if it takes four hours, you're going to get your money right here in front of everybody.'"

There was no question: NASCAR was there to stay.

"You know, of course, the best race every year was the one *to* Daytona, and not the one *at* Daytona." It was a bench-racing session after the 25th Anniversary NASCAR dinner, and the man talking was Jerome (Red) Vogt.

"Why, everybody from Atlanta—and that was a big part of the field, right there—would line up in front of my garage." he said, "and the tales would start, about last year's race or Lakewood or any place, but the bigger the tales got, the more fired up everybody became. And, when they all were there, the race began.

"They raced from the front of my place to Bill France's filling station in Daytona. Some of them drove their race cars and others towed them flat,

It was to be many years before Goodyear got into racing, but it came close as the traveling display visited Daytona and the service station of Frank Swain, who would become one of NASCAR's first starters.

A young Bill France awaits the start of the 1936 beach course race. France started tenth and finished fifth, driving a Ford.

behind all kinds of vehicles. How all of them made it, I don't know. But I guess it proved how well they could drive a car. Anywhere."

When they all arrived in Daytona on February 14, 1948, they found the biggest crowd of spectators ever for a beach race. More than 14,000 were on hand for the very first NASCAR-sanctioned event.

Cannonball Baker presided over the first driver's meeting, held at the Chamber of Commerce Building. They also held a drawing for starting positions.

After the drawing, rules were reviewed and much concern was expressed over the method of starting the race. For one thing, there was fear of a huge pileup in the South Turn on the first lap. So, for more than an hour drivers and officials expressed their opinions. During all the rhetoric, a lanky Greyhound bus driver from Atlanta, Jack Ethridge, stood in a corner of the crowded room and listened, saying nothing. Finally he raised his hand and was recognized by Baker. Jack's suggestion broke up the meeting.

NASCAR's *first super star, Bob "Red" Byron, won four consecutive beach course races between 1946 and 1949.*

"Why don't you just fire the gun and let us go? We know it's dangerous out there." he said.

And dangerous it was. The *Illustrated Speedway News* described it this way:

> *How the drivers escaped in one piece at the South Turn will always be a mystery to the fans who watched the race from that vantage point. It was at the sharply banked quarter of a mile South Turn which connects the beach and the road where the major crashes occurred.*
>
> *Ralph Sheeler was the first to miss the treacherous approach to the South Turn and go spilling over the edge of the bank into a sand dune pit 12 feet below. Tex Callahan smashed up on the eighth lap in the identical spot and landed kerplung atop Sheeler's car. In the 9th lap, Glenn Roberts missed the turn completely and capsized. Jack Ethridge, a star driver, lost control of his car at the deceptive South Turn in the 11th lap and hung on the edge of the sand drop. To make it a full house, Turk Atkins came barreling around the turn in the 54th lap and he, too, bashed into the other wrecked cars.*
>
> *The hole neighboring the South Turn resembled a junk yard, three of the cars upside down and demolished.*
>
> *One crackup at the North Turn occurred in the early phase of the race. Max French drove his car piggy-back on another speeding buggy and flipped over.*

While all this was taking place in the turns, there was even more action on the straightaways.

Marshall Teague started from the front row and took a commanding early lead, pulling out in front by nearly half a mile at one point. Fonty Flock made his bid, piloting the Number 1 car into the Number 1 position on the 35th lap. He built up a half-mile lead by Lap 49.

Racing down the road-backstretch flat out, Flock's right front spindle broke and the wheel flew off, causing the car to flip three times, into the palmettos.

With Fonty out, Teague commanded the race until the 53rd lap when Red Byron, who had been in hot pursuit all afternoon, took over. After that, it was simply the combination of smooth Byron driving and the race car of Red Vogt that spelled victory. Byron won his third straight beach course event.

Race reports show that Teague completed the entire 150-mile race without a pit stop, but ran out of gas as he crossed the finish line in second place.

One of the greatest feats of driving in the race was turned in by Bob Flock, who started 14th and was running a strong fourth by the end of 25 laps, when his motor blew. He flagged down J.F. Fricks, a fellow Atlantan, who was in ninth place and took over his car. He roared around the new 2.2-mile course and finished third.

There were only 12 cars running at the end.

It is appropriate in a way that the first NASCAR Grand National race was held in Charlotte. Bill France had gone there even before NASCAR was formed to talk with Wilton Garrison, sports editor of the *Charlotte Observer*, about publicity for a "national championship race" for the National Championship Stock Car Circuit.

"He asked me who was going to run in it," says France, "and I told him some of the names. Well, he said he could see how we might have a championship for the Carolinas and Georgia, but not a *national* championship, with that field.

"I asked him what he thought we needed to have a national championship, and he said we needed to establish a point fund and to have some continuity to our rules. It got me to thinking."

In this respect, it had been Charlotte where France had gotten the inspiration to form NASCAR. On June 19, 1949, he was back in Charlotte with a point fund made up of 7½ percent of the purse of each race, and a set of rules with a lot of continuity. He also had a $6,000 purse and an idea for racing *new* cars that was to roar to immediate acceptance with the fans. It was not called "Grand National" yet—that would come later—but it was the first Grand National race nevertheless.

Race day brought several problems. One of the major ones was a ten-mile long traffic jam, which, along with the thousands of fans, included most of the race cars, since they were *driven* to the race. It was, after all, a strictly stock car race.

Once the race cars got on the track, they created the second problem. Dust. The new Charlotte Speedway had been constructed with new cars in mind, but they had not reckoned on the three-quarter mile track becoming as dusty as it did. One observer said it looked like a "miniature A-bomb had gone off." The mushroom cloud of red dust reached a couple of hundred feet into the sky over southwest Charlotte, settling on nearby Wilkerson Boulevard. It caused several wrecks on the road, which was then the main thoroughfare between Charlotte and Gastonia and points south. The highway patrol appeared and told France that they were going to have to close down the track if they couldn't get the dust under control.

They found 50 bags of calcium chloride in a storage room under the stands that had been used for a motorcycle race, and they loaded it into a pick-up one of the fans provided. They worked the chemical into the turns by dumping it over the side of the truck and then dragging a piece of screen wire over it. Basic but effective.

"Easily the most intriguing part of the whole affair was how some of the drivers got their race cars," says Tuthill. "For example, Tim Flock spotted a couple watching practice from their brand new 1949 Olds 88, and, do you know, he actually talked them into letting him *race* it. He qualified third."

Lee Petty had planned a little more in advance. He had borrowed a 1948 Buick Roadmaster from a friend. He was sure the big straight-eight was fast enough and heavy enough to stick in the turns. Keep in mind, it was *strictly* stock, so the drivers couldn't even do anything to the suspension or shocks or anything. They had to depend on cars they knew to be good on the highway. "A heavy car will do just fine," Petty said.

Petty had taken the car out on the lonely backroads around his home in Randleman and raced everything in sight, "getting the feel of it," he said. Nobody knows how many races he had won with the car *before* he got to the track. Then he and his brother Julie tuned the car to within an inch of its life. And they painted a number 42 on the side of it. Those were the last two numbers in the license plate, so it was as good as any number, he reasoned. A relatively unromantic reason for choosing a number that was to become so famous.

Glenn Dunnaway, like Tim Flock, had come to the race without a ride. Helmet in hand, he asked Tuthill if anybody needed a driver.

"Yeah, Hubert Westmoreland over there. He's got a '47 Ford and needs a driver," he said. "It's probably a whiskey-runnin' car," he added.

"It wouldn't be the first time," Dunnaway said.

By the time everybody had begged, borrowed and maybe even stolen all the cars they could get, there were 32 "race cars" ready to compete.

The crowd of 13,000 roared its approval when the starter dropped the green flag, sending the 32 cars on their way. Bob Flock, starting from the pole, zipped into the lead in the first turn, trailed by Red Byron and the rest of the racing Flock family, Tim and Fonty. There were two relative newcomers to the NASCAR scene, right in there with the veterans: Curtis Turner, a whiskey-running timber man from Virginia, and Buck Baker, a

Gober Sosebee of Atlanta was one of the early beach course greats. He won two modified races there and was outstanding in Grand National competition.

Fonty Flock, one of the early NASCAR greats, displays an early summer driving suit.

Cotton Owens, left, race driver turned car-builder, and Buddy Baker, who was in his father's pit crew, watch qualifying on the beach.

Charlotte bus driver. Before the day was over, the names of Turner and Baker would be added to the list of Southern stock car heroes, and also the names of Julius (Tim) Flock and Lee Petty.

"Miraculously, the cars got through the first turn, and the first few laps," Petty says, "although there was some wild maneuvering for position. The cars were going wide, up near the fence, and down low in the grass infield. They were all over the track, trying to find a place where the car would stick."

As Bill France had predicted, the crowd loved it. And immediately, the Ford owners among the fans took up with the Fords on the track, cheering wildly for them. The Chevy owners united, as did the Plymouth owners. It was to be the major reason for the popularity of stock car racing in the South. The fans realized that the strictly stock cars were just like the ones they were driving. It was racing with which they could identify.

"A lot of wild things happened that day," says Petty. "One of the cars turned over in the infield in a clump of bushes and stirred up a nest of yellow jackets. The driver didn't get hurt in the crash, but the yellow jackets almost killed him before he got out of the car. Everybody figured the car was on fire the way he came running out of there. And, just as quickly as anyone would run over to see what was wrong, the yellow jackets would take after him. In a few minutes, there were people running all over the pits, and the fans, who couldn't see what was actually going on, thought everybody had lost their minds. They never did get that car back in the race."

Petty steadily moved up through the pack, and was about to take the lead when the radius rod broke on the Buick. That left him rolling along on four coil springs with nothing to hold it down. It got to bouncing so badly that it finally flipped. Four times. There were parts flying all over the track.

NASCAR's next big step came in a cotton field in the Pee Dee section of South Carolina, just outside of Darlington. On December 13, 1949, ground was broken on a paved mile and a quarter speedway. It was to be the first superspeedway in the world, designed for stock cars.

The first race was set for Labor Day 1950. For 500 miles! It was billed as a combination World Series and Kentucky Derby—stock car's answer to the Indianapolis 500.

The Central States Racing Association was chosen to sanction the race, even though they had doubts that stock cars could run 500 miles at high speeds. Bill France, however, did not share this skepticism.

"I had known Harold Brasington for a few years," says France, "because he had driven several races at the beach. He had a dream. He wanted to build this big track at Darlington. I had an appointment with him to discuss the thing at Hillsboro, Virginia, one time, but I couldn't fly in because of bad weather, and there were no telephones, so I couldn't talk it over with him right then.

"Then next thing I knew, he had bought property on the west side of Darlington and was beginning the thing. I really never expected them to finish it."

Construction continued but entries failed to come in for the race. Brasington again contacted France.

"Harold had been selling advance reserve tickets in order to finance the construction," France says, "and with two months left before the Labor Day race, he only had one entry. So he had two of his people, Bob Colvin and Barney Wallace, set up a meeting with me in Charlotte. After talking with them, I said I didn't think it would work. But they convinced me to go down and take a look.

"I went down there, and I was amazed," says France. "They had completed two-thirds of the first major facility for stock car racing in the nation, and already had sold over $25,000 worth of tickets. So we immediately switched the event to NASCAR, sent out a new entry blank and changed the starting field from 33 to 75 cars."

"There must have been 30,000 people there on race day," Tuthill recalls. "But we had gone down early. In fact, the real story began before we got there. Bill France, Curtis Turner, Alvin Hawkins and Johnny Mantz bought a new Plymouth sedan in Winston-Salem on the way to Darlington. They paid $1,700 for it; and they brought it just to get there and to have

Smokey Purser was usually the man to beat in post World War II beach racing.

Fireball Roberts was 18-years-old when this photo was taken in 1947. He went on to become one of NASCAR's greatest drivers.

Curtis Turner was one of NASCAR's *all-time favorites. His hard-driving style made him a standout in any pack of racers.*

something to run around in once we got down there.

"They figured they would either race it on a short track somewhere later or sell it. They really didn't know what they were going to do with it. But that car came in handy. It was always parked outside the Darlington Motel, and any time anybody needed to go after food or drinks or whatever, they took the little black Plymouth. We took it back and forth to the Elk's Club in Florence. Everywhere. It was our hack.

"Well, Mantz," Tuthill continues, "was a hot-shot Indy driver and he had come down to find a ride for the Southern 500. But, by the day before the race, he hadn't found one, so he came back to the motel, looking for the Plymouth."

"Where's the Plymouth?" he asked.

"I think somebody took it into town," I told him.

"Well, tell them to leave it here when they get back. I'm gonna' race it tomorrow. Remember, keep it here," he said.

"Wait," I said. "Run through that again. Particularly the part about racing it," I said.

"You heard me," Mantz said. "I'm gonna' race it."

"We weren't the only ones who thought he was crazy," says Tuthill. "Everybody did. Especially on race day. There were Oldsmobiles and Fords and Cadillacs and Lincolns. Everything. And here was Mantz in that six cylinder Plymouth.

"He had come up with some Indy Firestones and, at least, he was the only one in the race with anything that even remotely resembled racing tires. We all doubted that it would make up for the lack of horsepower," Tuthill says.

"But Mantz put on a show," he says. "He just drove around the track, way up high, at a steady pace all day—about 70 or 75 miles an hour—and he did everything right. He pitted under caution—which is something he had learned at Indy—and, generally, he made everybody else on the track madder than hell. Particularly after he got in the lead.

"Red Byron in Red Vogt's Cadillac and Fireball Roberts in an Olds 88 would blaze right by him and roar down the back stretch, and then KER-BOOM a tire would blow and into the pits they would go. And there would be Mantz, tooling along at 70, right through the turns and down the straight, right past the pits where everybody was frantically changing tires.

"One of the drivers said after the race that he knew exactly how many pit stops he had made. Twenty-seven. Because he counted the blown-out tires in his pit.

"When the checkered flag came down," Tuthill says, "Mantz had built up a two lap lead on the field. Everybody was in a state of shock. Especially Red Vogt. He was over at the garage where the car was being checked, and he kept saying, 'I know there's something phony. There's no way a Plymouth can beat a Cadillac. No way.'

"I told Al Crisler to check anything Red wanted checked, and I went back to the motel to have a drink and join the card game.

"The next morning I got a phone call from Al. 'How'd the inspection go?' I asked."

"Go? he said. "It's still *going*."

"It's *still* going on?" Tuthill asked in disbelief.

"Yeah," he said, "I think you'd better come over."

"When I got there," Tuthill chuckles, "Vogt was pacing the floor. Everything was torn apart—the carburetor, the exhaust, the heads. Everything. The pistons were out, the valves, even the gas tank was off. And the wheels and brakes. Red looked at me and said, 'There's no way a Plymouth can beat a Cadillac.'

"I looked around again and told Red that obviously everything had been taken apart, and that it was all there for him to see."

"I know, I can see," Vogt said, "But I'm still not satisfied. There's no way..."

"Yeah, I know," Tuthill said.

"Tut," Crisler said, "we've been to the Plymouth dealer four times. We got him out of bed *twice*. We compared valve springs and heads and carbs. We even compared the mill marks on the heads to see if they were turned in the right direction. Everything's off that will *come* off."

After another hour or so, they dumped all of the parts in the back seat of the Plymouth and declared Mantz the official winner of the first Southern 500. In the hack. But they never did convince Red Vogt that a Plymouth could outrun a Cadillac.

NASCAR was rolling.

With an eye toward the growing popularity of hot rod racing, they sanctioned a 100-mile national roadster championship on a two-mile paved area near Davie, Florida, that had served as an airfield during World War II. More than 20 entries came from the Chicago area alone, mostly because of Andy Granatelli, who was running regular roadster events at Soldier's Field. Granatelli brought two roadsters himself, one which he had bought in California. He billed it as "the world's fastest roadster."

Willie Sternquist drove the California roadster and Jim Rathman drove the other. About the only other car that was considered in the same league with the Granatelli cars was Red Vogt's nifty-looking '34 Ford. Bob Flock had the driving duties.

"Granatelli told Sternquist to race with Flock," France says, "fully expecting his car to run Vogt's right into the ground. That way his cars would run one and two. So, when the flag was dropped, Sternquist and Flock took off, leading everybody. They set such a pace that both lapped Rathman. Then something happened that Andy hadn't planned on: Sternquist's roadster blew. It couldn't keep pace with Vogt's car.

"Well, when Willie's engine let go, Andy gave Rathman the "go" sign, but it was too late," says France. "There was no way he could make up a full lap on Flock. After the race, Granatelli came to me and said, 'That's the last time I'm ever gonna' try to win a race by using strategy.' "

NASCAR followed the roadster show by fully organizing the sportsman, modified and straightaway beach divisions. And they increased racing on the beach from one week to two.

Daytona Beach, 1955—Gentleman Jim Kimberly in his Ferrari; Paul Whiteman at far right.

Harry LeDuc flags a Jaguar in straightaway activity on the beach as a mile-long line of cars await their turn.

"Ferrari, Jaguar, Mercedes and other high-priced imports shared the Measured Mile with domestic brands, ranging from Studebaker Champions to Cadillac Eldorados in straightaway runs," Tuthill says. "There were enough classes and trophies to satisfy anyone who thought he could win one in high speed or acceleration. But, late every night, they staged impromptu drags, just for the heck of it, like they had always done.

"These clandestine meetings started about midnight and went until dawn, far down the beach. They had no organization, no rules, no publicity and certainly no advertising, except for word-of-mouth. Yet hundreds of unsanctioned competitors showed up, and had a ball. That is, until we came in with officials, rules and regulations, and a desire to make the whole thing legal. Many of the first entrants in our 'official' runs were irked with the red tape and comparative formality and delays, so they drove back up the beach to Main Street and started their own contests," Tuthill says.

"This brought out the police and firemen with hoses and, in short order, a full-blown riot was taking place. Bill France really had his hands full in dragging racing into respectability."

The idea of the straightaway runs in the first place was to bring back some of the activity of the old days, so when France went to the city fathers, they promised some financial aid. Tuthill went to California to talk with some of the hot dogs out there about coming back East to race. One of the first to agree to come was Bill Dailey with the streamliner So-Cal Special. He was also one of the first to crash.

To make the runs official, it was necessary to use the city's timing device that had been used for the Campbell runs, but for some reason the AAA had gotten hold of it to time the runs at the Salt Flats, and they had never returned it.

"It was the only one around at the time," France says, "that would stamp the time on a tape, so we demanded it back. And we got it—after paying the AAA for keeping it calibrated. But we paid it and told the world that the world famous Daytona timer was back in operation."

Drivers showed up by the hundreds; many of them only wanted the certificate, showing that they had been timed on the "World's Most Famous Beach." Those that went over 100 miles per hour became members of the

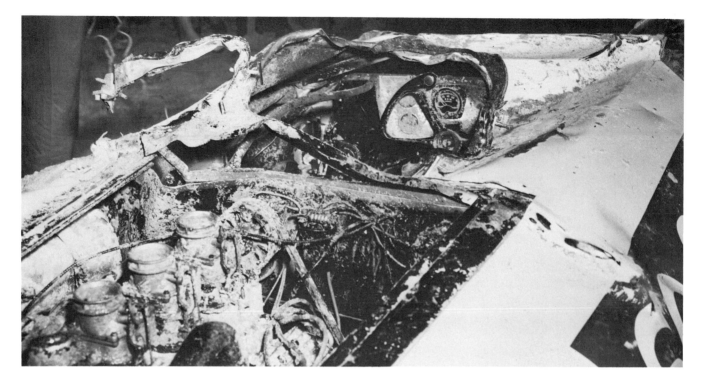

Century Club. Joe Littlejohn was the first to drive a U.S. stock passenger car over 100 miles per hour. He turned 100.28 in his '50 Olds.

The straightaway runs also gave officials a chance to qualify cars for the beach-road course races. Rutting sand was still a problem, so there was no practice or qualifying on the course, they simply used the beach timer on straightaway speed runs. Once again, there was plenty of activity on the beach.

In fact, there was a lot happening *throughout* NASCAR.

"We were traveling all over the country," Tuthill says, "and, even though racing was beginning to take on a little more sophistication at the Beach, there still were places where it was a little rough. I shared a room up

Bill Dailey survived the 175 mile per hour crash of the So-Cal Special in the 1951 Speed Weeks.

Long before electronic devices and sophisticated scoring techniques, this is what the scoring stand looked like for a NASCAR race.

70

in North Wilkesboro with Alvin Hawkins, who was one of our first starters, and, when he got up in the morning and put his clothes on, he reached into the dresser drawer and got a .38 revolver and stuck it in his belt. 'What the hell is that for?' I asked him. 'Just standard equipment for a starter around here,' he said."

And Joe Epton, who was NASCAR's first scorer, tells of the time when a man came into the scorer's stand and laid a shotgun on the table, proclaiming, "I got a car in that race, and I jus' wanna' make sure you're doin' it right."

"It was a slow process," says Tuthill. "Even safety. At first, I went to a surplus store in Jacksonville and bought those old army safety belts by the carton—paid fifty cents a pair for them—and I'd take them to the tracks and sell them for a dollar a pair, or, at times, I'd give them to a driver if he didn't have the money. I did the same thing with helmets. I got a bunch of old British dispatch helmets, just like the old Cromwells and Seagraves, you know, with the high domes, and I sold them to a lot of the guys. They were

Bill Snowden thrilled stock car fans on the beach. Note the football helmet he—and many others—used as a crash helmet.

Tim Flock, wearing a Cromwell-type crash helmet, awaits the start of the 1956 convertible race. He won the convertible race the following year.

as good as the football helmets a lot of them were wearing."

"We tested some safety products for the cars, too," Tuthill added. "Bill France would bring his car out to the beach and we would put something like air lift shocks on it and test it, comparing it to mine with standard shocks. It wasn't the most elaborate test, but we were trying to make it all safer. I mean, those were the times when a lot of drivers still strapped their doors shut with a belt or a piece of rope. They only had a single roll bar, and completely stock interiors. All the seats and everything. Radios, sun visors."

But, little by little, the sport was developing into one of skill and finesse. Drivers were beginning to attract huge followings, and definite styles were developing. It wasn't any secret, however, that some of them still came from the "moonshine school of driving." Like Junior Johnson, who came out of the hills of North Carolina, probably with a revenuer after him. Johnson was to become legendary as both a race driver and a wit. An example of his homespun humor took place in the first season he ever ran NASCAR. Johnson was talking with Bill France, shortly after he had completed his third Grand National race. The conversation went something like this:

"Junior, you're doing well and we expect you to run all 30 races this season," said France.

"No, Bill, I'm only gonna' run a few of them," replied Johnson.

"But you're committed, Junior."

"No, Bill, what it is, I'm *involved*," Johnson quipped.

"You're committed, Junior," said France, a little more sternly.

Junior looked at him for a moment, and then he drawled: "Bill, you've just got the words all wrong. Now, lissen, if you sit down to breakfast tomorrow to bacon and eggs, the chicken is *involved*. The pig is *committed*."

End of conversation. Johnson ran his few races.

But would anybody like to pick the best *driver* of the beach course days? It's not likely.

"You couldn't pick a 'best driver' because there were so many different

The fierce series of flips by Junior Johnson in the Pontiac was typical of beach action. Johnson, who apparently decided he had had enough of the thrill show, departs via the back window before the final roll.

styles," says Tuthill. Herb Thomas, for instance, was one of the best drivers ever. In *any* period. I mean, if he were around racing today, he would be a millionaire. And for sheer skill, Tim Flock was hard to beat. First thing off, he would try to get out front and he would always try to get the second place man in sight, and would work on getting a lap on him. He wouldn't try to pass him; he just stayed right behind him. And he worried him. How he ever got the lap in the first place, nobody knew. But he could do it more often than not.

"And Paul Goldsmith, why, he would go into the South Turn faster than almost anybody. His momentum seemed to carry him right through the

Herb Thomas "steps down" into his Hudson race car as Cannonball Baker, left, and Smokey Yunick (with derby instead of the familiar ten-gallon-type trademark). Frank Swain is the starter.

Bill France, at passenger door, and Curtis Turner, at driver's door, prepare for the start of the 1950 Mexican Road Race. They won the race but were disqualified for changing cars—from one team Nash to another—during the race.

turn and out onto the beach. Fireball did the same thing. I mean you just didn't think either of them were going to make it. They would fly out of the turn and past six or eight guys going up the beach.

"Fonty was good," Tuthill recalls, gazing off into the past. "He was in perfect control at all times, even if he was backwards. He always seemed to know exactly where the car was going.

"Then there was Curtis Turner. He was like a mythical character. He didn't always win, but you could pick him out of a pack of 20 cars. Here he would come down the beach, and he would *throw* the car sideways and just hold it there through the turn. He was hard on equipment, but he made good lap times. Bob Flock was the same way. They both just plowed through traffic. In the turns.

"The stories of Curtis and Bill France in the Mexican Road Race were something," Tuthill says. It must have been some ride. They were in one of the Nash team cars. Curtis lost his brakes coming out of the mountains and he was slowing it down by dragging the front against rocks and piles of sand and dirt. At over a hundred miles an hour. They took over the other Nash and won, but they were disqualified because you weren't supposed to switch cars.

"There were lots of good drivers in those days," he says. "Buck Baker and Lee Petty and Joe Weatherly. A lot of them. Marshall Teague was both a good driver and a good mechanic, but he was pretty uncooperative. Most of the other guys weren't."

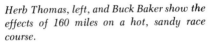

Herb Thomas, left, and Buck Baker show the effects of 160 miles on a hot, sandy race course.

A field of more than 70 modifieds roar to a start up the beach straightaway.

The beach course era was in high gear in 1949. The official program even listed *odds* for the various drivers, with Red Byron and Fonty Flock going to the pole as the favorites at 4 to 1, followed at 6 to 1 by Tim and Bob Flock, Curtis Turner and Buddy Shuman. Fireball Roberts, still pretty new to the sport, was 18 to 1.

The oddsmakers knew what they were doing. Red Byron won his *fourth straight* beach course event, this time in a new 1949 Olds 88. The cars had switched to the 4.1-mile course that had been designed for the bikes. They never again ran on the 2.2-mile course—it was too slow for them.

The Olds victory broke a Ford dominance of the beach and ushered in an era that saw manufacturers getting involved. The fans, too, took great interest in the late model cars, because it was the first time most got to see the new models.

The early races did not, however, make Detroit look good at all times. The stock machines broke wheels, collapsed front ends, and did a variety of other things that made them appear "weak." So NASCAR began to allow the drivers to beef up wheels and improve shocks and suspensions. It was not to alter the stock characteristics, but rather to provide a wider margin of safety for the drivers and fans.

Nineteen-fifty-one may have been something entirely different to the Chinese, but to NASCAR it was the year of the Hornet. In fact, it opened the *era* of the Hornet, a period when Hudsons were as close to being unbeatable as any car ever has been. Marshall Teague was the first hot Hudson pilot, winning in '51 and '52.

Marshall Teague, ready for 1952 Daytona action.

Adhesion between street tires and the sand wasn't always maximum, as evidenced by the remains of an Olds 88 on the beach straightaway.

It was also a period when factories not only got into the scene, but they began to take a few extra steps to win. Sometimes outside the rules.

"The drivers didn't start the cheating, the factories did," says Tuthill. "Actually the drivers operated under a strange code, despite how wild they were. They would rather beat somebody honestly. But the factory cars had all sorts of innovations, from disappearing fan belts to extra engine blocks in

In the Fifties, after the factories got involved, Bill France tried to avoid controversy by having a "rules" meeting before the racing started. Shown here, l to r: Chuck Daigh, Ford; Walter McKenzie, Chevrolet; Dick Dolan, Pure Oil; Vince Piggins, Chevrolet; Betty Skelton, Chevrolet; and Peter DePaolo, Ford.

A trio of Flocks and a pair of Chryslers. From left, Fonty, Bob and Tim Flock were among NASCAR's greatest early stars. Their records stood for many years.

A Smokey Yunick car, a Fish carburetor and a young Fireball Roberts was a tough combination to beat in 50s modified racing.

the trunks for added weight.

"A lot of the cars were brought here by dealers. They would tow them—or sometimes drive them—down here, hire a driver, and then take them back and put them on their used car lots after the race.

"It was a period when a lot of cars became popular because of racing at the beach and at Darlington," says Tuthill. "Lincoln did well here (Harold

Kite won the 1950 beach race in one) and the Olds 88. But usually the big cars showed a weakness because they used a lot of the same parts as the Chevys and Fords and Plymouths. A certain bearing, for instance, that was used in a Chevy, might also be used right up through the GM line, and, naturally, it would hold up under racing strains a lot longer in the lighter Chevy than it would in, say, a Cadillac. It's why everybody always said that if Lee Petty could race long enough in his Plymouth, he would win."

Teague had proved the Hudson in 1951 and 1952, but Olds retaliated with some new and hotter stuff in 1953, with Bill Blair winning. Fonty was second in another Olds. The Chrysler took over with Lee Petty and Tim Flock winning all the marbles for the next three years—with a little help from the rules committee. Tim was flagged the winner in 1954 in his Olds, but the inspection revealed soldered carburetor butterflies, giving the race to Lee. The following year, Tim got it back when Fireball Roberts, in a Buick, crossed the finish line in front but was disqualified because of an "alteration to the push rods." Tim repeated in 1956, without any help, as he edged Billy Myers.

"During this period, Tuthill says, "outboard engine manufacturer Carl Kiekhaefer entered the picture with the first regimented money-is-no-object effort, and a team of Chrysler cars, driven by Speedy Thompson, Tim and Fonty Flock, Buck Baker and Frank Mundy.

"But it was in 1952 that one of the wildest things happened involving a

Lee Petty slides through the North Turn, on his way to victory in 1954. It was the first of three consecutive Chrysler victories on the beach course.

The fabulous Hudson Hornet reigned supreme in NASCAR racing for several years. Marshall Teague won the beach course races in 1951 and 1952 in this one.

factory team," says Tuthill. "Teague and Jim Rathman had *carte blanche* privileges at the Hudson plant. In fact, Teague was the first driver ever to get factory sponsorship because he was the one who developed the dual intake manifold for the Hudson, which they later marketed as 'Twin-H Power.' So Teague and Rathman showed up for a race with the new carb setup and said it was a factory option.

"I asked to see the spec sheet on it, and Teague pulled one out. Well, it was so fresh, the ink was smeared. He said more of the manifolds would be there the next day, for the rest of the Hudsons. But the manifolds didn't arrive, so I cornered Marshall and asked him about it. 'Aw, I should have told you, Tut,' he said. 'All those other manifolds were on a cart at the plant and some guy upset it and broke 'em all. 'Cept these two Jim and me got.' They ran that first race without the Twin-H Power. But it didn't slow Hudson down at all. They were determined to win.

"Some genius at Hudson found out that if you took a Hudson Wasp head and put in on the Hornet *backwards,* all of the bolt holes would match

up. And, since no new holes had to be drilled, it met NASCAR rules. It also raised the compression to 11 to 1. I went up to the Hudson people," Tuthill says, "and I told them that the engines were going to heat up on short, dusty tracks and blow, but they said, 'We want to win, and we're using them. They're legal.' They used them, and most of the engines heated up and blew.

"They went right back to the drawing board," he says. "But Hudson wasn't alone. The Chrysler 300s had aluminum roll bars and lightened bodies and trick tires. And Olds even changed their suspension because of racing. It was an interesting period.

"If you were caught cheating, you lost your points," Tuthill points out, "but the factories didn't care because most people would still think they won

Bill Blair won the 1953 beach course race in an Olds 88 with a record speed of 89.50 miles per hour.

The Kiekhaffer Chrysler 300s were the pride and joy of NASCAR for a long time. Here Buck Baker pauses after qualifying for a beach race.

anyway. All the fans left the track, thinking a Ford had won, and the newspapers carried the story saying Ford had won, so in their minds forever after, a Ford won. Even if it had been disqualified. It was a calculated risk the factories—most of them—took.

"We got almost no support from the factories, unless it was in their own interest," Tuthill says. "There were times when the factories were really interested in showcasing their products—by winning at Daytona."

L to r: Dick Dolan, Pure Oil Co., Speedy Thomspon, and Ed Otto, NASCAR official, in Daytona 1957 Victory Circle.

The narrow North Turn was the scene of many crashes. In this 1955 modified race, six separate crashes occurred in the turn.

The starting field rounds the North Turn and heads down the road section.

Wally Parks, who was to become president of the National Hot Rod Association, roars through the traps on the beach in 1957 in an experimental Plymouth. His top speed in the measured mile was 166.89 miles per hour.

Ralph Moody starts to flip as Lee Petty goes by on the inside of the old beach course.

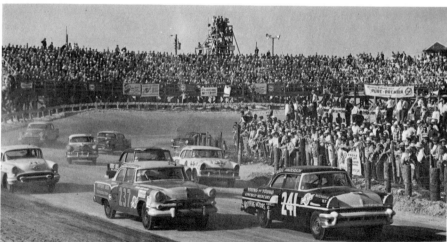

Part of the field coming out of the South Turn and lining up for the start of the 1955 race.

Smoke from the fatal Alfred Briggs North Turn crash in the 1955 modified race can be seen all the way to the South Turn. The four-car pileup stopped the race.

Four early NASCAR heroes, from left to right, Tim Flock, Lee Petty, Buck Baker and Junior Johnson await qualifications for the 1955 beach course race, which, incidentally, Flock won.

Joe Weatherly, 12, roars past Jimmy Thompson in the North Turn in 1957 convertible race action.

Paul Goldsmith on the beach in a Smokey Yunick Chevrolet convertible.

North Turn modified action.

Joe Weatherly, 12, and Lee Petty exchange paint in frantic convertible action.

February, 1951, from the back of the north turn grandstand, looking south.

The famous broadsliding style of Curtis Turner on the old beach course.

Curtis Turner in top-down comfort at the beach.

Darel Diereinger in one of his early convertible rides.

Herb Thomas, one of the early NASCAR greats, examines a racing slick that wasn't exactly designed that way.

Miss Dianne Davis, right, of Chicago, presenting tropht to Cotton Owens, winner of the Daytona Beach 100-mile sportsmen's and modified championship race February, 1953. Ralph Moody, second place finisher, looks on.

Starter Frank Swain watches, Bill France gets ready to drive and Smokey Yunick lends a hand in straightaway runs.

(LEFT TO RIGHT)
Frank Mundy, twice National AAA Stock Car Racing Champion (1953 & 1955), Lee Petty, 1954 National Champion and Bill France, President of NASCAR made a guest appearance on the Dodge sponsored "Break the Bank" TV show. Here they tell Bert Parks and the national TV audience about the 250-mile International Road Race to be run over the "Road American" course. Both Mundy and Petty will drive Dodge D-500's in this event which is under the direction of Bill France.

Bill France, left, and automotive writer Tom McCahill prepare to advertise the 1954 beach race.

Bill Frick in 4.9 litre Ferrari, Daytona Beach, February 1955.

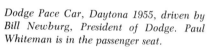

Bill France flags Phil Walters in the D-type Jaguar in a 1955 straightaway run.

Dodge Pace Car, Daytona 1955, driven by Bill Newburg, President of Dodge. Paul Whiteman is in the passenger seat.

Victory Circle, 1955, Tim Flock and family.

Daytona Beach 1955, l to r: Ed Rutherfurd, Jack Rutherfurd, Dick Dolan, Briggs Cunningham, Phil Walters and Ed Otto.

One of America's earliest woman race drivers, Betty Skelton, pauses with Bill France and the 1956 Pace Car. Miss Skelton held speed records on the land, in the air and on water.

From left, former Indianapolis-driver Ira Vail, Bill Tuthill, Cannonball Baker and Darlington P.R. chief Rus Catlin chat at Tuthill's Museum of Speed in 1957.

Daytona Beach 1956—Banjo Matthews is ready to go.

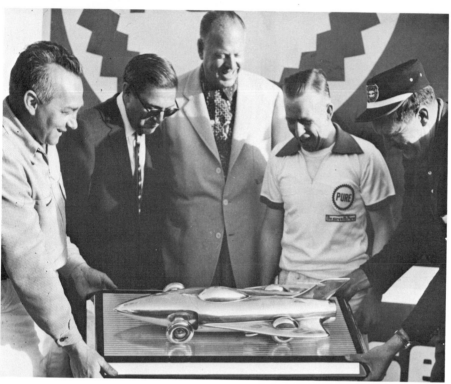

L to r: Ray Nichels, Semon Knudsen, Harley Earl, Cotton Owens, and Bill France, Sr. looking at Firebird styling car, Daytona 1957.

Mauri Rose testing GM Firebird at Daytona Beach, 1957.

Daytona 1957: Victory Circle, l to r, Joe Weatherly, Tim Flock and Bill France, Sr.

Joe Weatherly and Curtis Turner before 125 mile modified race, Daytona 1957.

Daytona 1958: Four national champions—Ned Jarrett, Jim Reed, Buck Baker (shaking hands with Harry Meyer) and Bob Wilborn.

Vince Piggins and his engineers at Chevrolet realized the high speed potential of the new Chevy V-8 in 1955 and brought the "hot one" to the attention of a new generation, although they never won a big event on the beach. A Smokey Yunick-prepared Chevy with ex-motorcycle rider Paul Goldsmith at the wheel came the closest. He was way out in front in 1957 when the engine blew. Cotton Owens scored a surprise victory for Pontiac.

During the same period, Ford got back into the picture with a team managed by former Indy great Peter DePaolo, with help from John Holman and Ralph Moody, who would later inherit the Ford racing program.

The final race on the beach in 1958 was perhaps the best of them all. After many crashes and lead changes, Goldsmith took over. He built up nearly a one-mile lead over Curtis Turner and, as they reached the last lap, it appeared to be all over. Goldsmith roared up the beach and waved to Smokey in the pits, but the racing strip was narrowed to two car widths by the incoming tide, and when Goldie pulled out to pass some slower cars, he hit a slough. The car was engulfed in salt water spray. Blinded, Goldsmith drove straight ahead and right past the North Turn. When he realized what had happened, he spun the car around and thundered back down the beach, jumping over the lower lip of the turn and cutting off Turner. He beat Turner across the finish line by a car length.

"That final decade of beach-road racing brought stock cars from rags to riches," says Tuthill, "and it opened a whole new dimension. It was a time of fun, excitement and fond memories; an unforgettable experience. It was an unusual course that bred unusual happenings. It changed from year to year due to the action of the wind and the tides, often from lap to lap because of the pounding of a stampede of race cars.

"During the few hours the tide was out, a public highway was transformed into a racecourse. Cars and people moved down the beach and the roadway in a steady stream, watched the race, and then got back out again before being swamped by the incoming tide.

"Where else," asked Tuthill, "has there ever been a race course posted with signs saying 'Beware of Rattlesnakes?' Or where spectators, anchoring their boats in the surf, fished, drank beer and watched a thrilling race for free."

The third era of auto racing on Daytona Beach had passed. Race fans will never again experience the joys of sitting in the North Grandstands as a hundred race cars thunder down the beach and broadslide into the North Turn. They will miss lining the fence on the inside of the track as two solid miles of race cars roar down the paved roadway and blast into the South Turn. It was racing's greatest show. And one of it's most glorious moments.

The curtain did not come down on motorcycle racing for two more years, and in the 19-year span that the bikes raced on the beach, some of the greatest names in two-wheel racing came into being. There were names like Joe Leonard and Paul Goldsmith, who both went on to four-wheelers and dramatic careers at Indianapolis. The Daytona 200 also had a long list of promoters, ranging from the City of Daytona to Bill France to the Central Labor Union, and finally to Bill Tuthill for the last two years when nobody else would take it.

"The final bike runnings on the beach-road course," says Tuthill, were both won by Brad Andres and allowed him to share an honor previously held by only one person, triple winner Dick Kalmfoth.

"No one can ever share Paul Goldsmith's unique position on the beach," says Tuthill. "In 1953 Goldsmith halted a four year domination of foreign-made machines by riding a Harley-Davidson to victory. Five years later he drove a Pontiac home in front in that thrilling last Grand National event to become the only man in history to ever win the two big ones on Daytona Beach."

From the start of the Winton-Olds contest in 1902 to the dropping of the checkered flag on Andres fifty-eight years later, there were thousands of miles of racing tire prints left in the sand from Ormond to the inlet. Hundreds of speed marks were recorded and the greatest speed on earth was established there 14 times.

"Speed was, and always will be, the yardstick by which performance and engineering achievement is measured," says Tuthill.

"But speed and an ever-increasing press of population has forced the cars from the beach. As early as 1953, Bill France told city fathers that the end was in sight, that the cars were going too fast for the sand and that they had gone as far down the beach as they could go to escape the rush of new building.

By 1955 France had formed the Daytona Beach Motor Speedway Corporation and the State of Florida had developed a Speedway Authority to assist in building a proposed ultra-modern racing facility near the Daytona

Airport. On October 18, 1955, the *Daytona Beach Morning Journal* matter-of-factly reported the following:

A 'before' shot of the Daytona International Speedway, showing the dog racing track and the vast expanse beyond that was to become the speedway.

> *A lease between the city and Speedway District on 377 acres of airport property got final City Commission approval last night. It will become effective after the CAA approves it and the Authority sells the revenue bonds necessary to build the proposed two and a half mile auto race track.*
>
> *Under the terms of the 99-year lease, the district will pay the city $4,700 a year plus a percentage of the excess revenue. The rent will begin when the speedway is completed.*
>
> *For the first 10 years, in addition to the initial rental fee, the district will pay the city 10 percent of the revenue it receives from the Daytona Beach Motor Speedway Corp. in excess of the first $200,000. The initial yearly payment from the corporation will go to retire revenue certificates. The corporation has a contract with the district for operating the speedway part of the year.*
>
> *Headed by France, NASCAR president, the corporation has agreed to pay $225,000 rent a year on the track. Yesterday France said confidently: 'The track is going to be a fabulous success. The main thing I'm worried about is getting started. Once we do, we'll go,' he declared.*

The original members of the Daytona Beach Racing and Recreational Facility District—Tom Cobb, Secretary-Lawyer, J. Saxton Lloyd-Chairman, Dr. A.M. McCarthy, Dan Warren, Grady Williamson and James Horton—did a lot of work towards making it (the speedway) become a reality.

It is not easy to bring such a major project into reality, and the struggle Bill France endured was mirrored in the pages of the local newspapers for four years before construction actually began. Let us take a look at the chronological story from the pages of the *Daytona Beach Morning Journal* and *The Evening News*:

March 18, 1953—NASCAR officials announce the end is in sight for use of the existing beach and road course because of the increasing construction of new homes in the area.

March 25—Worried C. of C. asks Bill France for suggestions to continue the Daytona Beach traditional events.

April 4—France proposes construction of a million dollar speedway.

April 22—Mayor and City Commission ask State Legislature to create a racing authority.

December 13—Lou Perini, owner of the Milwaukee Braves, shows interest in building the speedway project. Cost now estimated at $1,675,000.

March 13, 1954—Perini and associates visit the site, after receiving the VIP treatment, with band music, pretty girls and Daytona hospitality. Perini orders thorough research and says he will consider nothing but the best racing plant in the World. $3,000,000 if needed, he says.

June 4—Perini drops plans when his engineers advise that the highway facilities are inadequate to handle anticipated traffic for the "World's biggest and best."

August 17—City and county appoint members of Legislature-created Racing Authority.

August 27—Authority accepts the proposal of a Cincinnati bond house to handle sale of revenue bonds for financing track construction. Firm guarantees to sell the bonds.

September 14—France says he will promote races on the beach course to maintain the continuity, but for just "one more time."

September 23—City leases land to Authority for 99 years, subject to approval of Civil Aeronautics Authority.

October 28—*Indianapolis Star* labels it a "pipe dream speedway."

November 5—Authority rejects plans calling for expenditure of three and half million dollars.

January 12, 1955—Authority calls for bids from prospective lessees.

February 12—Authority accepts the bid of Bill France, only one submitted, in which France agrees to deposit $200,000 annual rental in advance.

April 15—France goes to New York to meet with financial advisers to complete his promotional organization.

April 24—Authority reports AAA Contest Board will refuse to issue any sanction for speedway cars if France's corporation is the operator.

April 28—France agrees that advance rental deposit be increased to $400,000. Authority asks Legislature for bill to back up revenue bonds with the property tax valuation.

May 5—Reported that track will be built by October, 1956.

June 3—Governor signs speedway property tax guarantee bill.

June 7—France's corporation and Authority sign operation agreement, with $400,000 advance rent to be posted. Cost of track now estimated at $2,500,000. France predicts track ready July 4, 1957.

June 11—CAA balks at land use plans because of radio transmitter and runways at adjoining municipal airport.

June 21—Politics threaten to slow speedway plans, but city officials agree to back away from tampering with Authority.

September 21—J. Saxton Lloyd, Authority chairman, anticipates track will be in operation in 1957.

October 25—Defense Dept. okays land lease. Waiting CAA approval.

November 9—County starts to build new highways to serve the speedway.

December 15—CAA approval of lease is given. Lloyd repeats prediction it will be built in 1957.

December 30—City again formalizes the lease of the land in accord with CAA requirements. Bond issue now set at $2,900,000. Rental now advanced to $225,000 a year. France agrees in exchange for other considerations.

April 22, 1956—Authority begins bond issue validation proceedings.

July 17—County plans additional road construction to serve speedway.

August 1—Supreme Court approves bond issue validation.

September 5—Sixty contractors ask for chance to bid on construction out of 240 firms sampled by Authority.

October 8—Plans ready to be advertised for bids.

November 21—Tight money market stalls speedway plans. Interest rates soar out of reach because of school and highway bond issues flooding nation's markets.

April 19, 1957—Authority exhausts all financing possibilities except for general obligation bond issue, with public referendum.

May 8—Path is cleared for referendum, backed by C. of C. Election scheduled for September 17.

May 16—Taxpayers' groups ask for referendum delay.

Throughout May—Debate flourishes almost daily. Plans for referendum finally postponed until after February, 1958 Speed Weeks.

October 30—Speedway District (name has been changed from Authority) drops bombshell with announcement it has almost concluded arrangements with Bill France to lease the land, with France to build two and a half mile speedway, more than half million dollars to start, deferring construction of some grandstands and buildings as planned originally. November 8 is set as the deadline for other interested groups to "put up or shut up."

November 7—C. of C., after full study of reported sources of private financing for the full project, approves the District-France proposal.

November 8—France and Lloyd sign the agreement. France posts $27,000 advance rent for a 50 year land lease, with a 25 year renewal option.

Conclusion: The District sells the standing timber for $2,500 and the land clearing is under way.

Bill France says the speedway will be in operation early in 1959.

The following day, November 9, 1957, France presented his plans for the first "500-mile national championship late model stock car race on a new paved two and one-half mile speedway to be held 475 days from today."

Before the ink was dry on the contract he signed, leasing a 446 acre site from the Speedway District, France made a formal announcement:

We are organizing the Daytona Beach International Speedway Corp. which will begin construction within 30 days on an automobile race track to cost an estimated $750,000.

The first event will be a NASCAR *sanctioned 500 mile late model stock car race in 1959 on George Washington's birthday, February 22.*

The track will be the fastest in the country, supporting speed up to 200 miles per hour.

The plant will have 10,000 permanent seats plus temporary bleachers. There will be standing room in the infield (same as Indianapolis).

The plans are designed so that the speedway can be expanded and it is my goal in the future to more than triple the seating and, correspondingly, improve the racing facilities.

The international safety and speed trials on the beach straightaway will be continued in conjunction with the racing activities at the speedway. But the last 160 mile event on the present 3.2 mile beach-road track will be February 23, 1958. All future races will be at the speedway.

In addition to the annual 500 mile Winter stock car classic, a Summer stock car event will be at the speedway, probably on July 4.

Plans also call for building a winding sports car course around the infield of the speedway. Target date for the sports car course is 1961.

On January 8, 1958, the Daytona Beach International Speedway Corporation held its first organizational meeting, and issued the following statement:

William H. G. France has officially been elected president of the new corporation.

Other officers are: Muse Womack, vice president; Mrs. W. H. France, secretary-treasurer; W. O. Briggs, Jr., Mike Womer, Don Kendall, Paul Whiteman, Tom McCahill, Emory Thames, Aubrey Vincent, and William C. France, directors.

The Corporation has started work on a two and one-half mile automobile race track at an estimated cost of $750,000. The site is adjacent to the Municipal Airport.

France, in a progress report, said yesterday that preliminary work is going on schedule. Bulldozers have already cleared 75 of the 250 acres that will be used immediately. Construction of the racing plant itself will begin as soon as the land is cleared. The speedway is scheduled to be ready for the first national championship 500 mile stock car race on Washington's Birthday, February 22, 1959.

The organization meeting yesterday was in the First Atlantic National Bank. Plans for the sale of stock were studied and will be announced soon.

Bill France is president of NASCAR, *world's largest stock car racing organization, with headquarters in this city. Womack owns and operates the Womack Asphalt Construction Co. Briggs, of Detroit, directs the trust funds for the Briggs Automotive family. Womer, New York City, is a Time Magazine executive. Kendall, New York City, is president of the International Division of Pepsi-Cola. Whiteman, New York City, is a famed television and radio personality. McCahill, of Glen Gardner, New Jersey, is automobile editor of Mechanix Illustrated. Thames is president of the First Atlantic National Bank in this city. Vincent is City Attorney, and W. C. France is a* NASCAR *executive.*

Houston Lawing, of Greensboro, North Carolina, public relations director for Bill France Enterprises, was named an honorary director of the speedway.

The new 2.5 tri-oval was underway. It would have two steeply banked turns of 31 degrees—"as steep as they could lay asphalt," France says,—and a third turn, right in the middle of the front straightaway, forming a sort of triangle.

"I wanted our stock cars to be as fast as the Indianapolis cars, and with the high banking, that seemed possible," France says. "And I asked our engineer, Charles Moneypenny, to design the turns as flat planes, instead of the bowl-shaped designs they had in Europe. This way cars could run in more than one groove, and could pass in the turns just as easy as on the straightaway.

"We had spent two million dollars between the time the first tree was knocked down and we had the speedway completed," says France. "Which I didn't have the year before. I borrowed $600,000, ordered four steel and wood grandstands from Reeves Steel in Tampa and started selling tickets. And we used the ticket money for construction just as fast as it came in.

"We still ended up owing a lot of money to various people, so I went around and signed notes with them and even put up some of my stock as collateral. But we got it all paid off within five years after we opened the track.

"It wasn't easy," France recalls. "And there were a lot of good friends that helped. People like Griffith and Charlie Moneypenny, local engineers in Daytona that drew up plans on the basis that if the bonds were sold that they would get the engineering work.

On November 8, 1957, this happy group of NASCAR employees celebrates the signing of the lease agreement between the Daytona Beach Racing and Recreational Facility District and the Speedway Corporation for the purpose of constructing the speedway. Standing, l to r: Norris Friel, Walter Robinton, Jeanette Grasso, Ann Slack, Dee Common, Jane Parker, Bill France, Sr., Ruth Parsons, Dorothy Beech, Judy Jones, Ann Kerr, Helen Agness, Thea Loe, Al Kaye, and Pat Purcell; kneeling, l to r: Mel Larson and Al Smiles.

Bill France ponders the blueprints as clearing begins for the Daytona International Speedway.

Installation of the tunnel to the infield during 1958 construction of the Daytona International Speedway.

Sand is dredged out of what was to become Lake Lloyd in the Daytona infield. The sand was used in the banking for the turns.

The smoothed-out sand awaits asphalt as construction continues on the speedway.

Laying asphalt in the first turn during speedway construction.

The newly-completed Daytona International Speedway in 1959.

Also, Lou Perini had his New York architectural firm do a feasibility study on the project.

France had met Clint Murchison, Jr., a top sportsman and business man in the United States, who now owns the Dallas Cowboys, and explained to him the Speedway that he was trying to put together. Murchison asked that any plans be sent to him as he also owned a construction company, which at the time was doing a large construction job in Oriente Provence in Cuba. Murchison mentioned that he was having trouble—Castro had told his engineers to stop working on the job or they would shoot them and Batista had told them that if they did stop working on the job they would get shot.

"We had gotten to the point of moving the million yards of dirt to make the high bank track or just building a conventional 2 1/2 mile road, which would have cost mush less money." France then call Murchison back in Texas to find out if he had gotten his earth moving machinery out of Cuba. He apparently had but sent one of his top executives, Howard Sluyter, over to help France with his problems.

"If it had not been for Clint Murchison and Howard Sluyter we never would have accomplished the job of building the Speedway as it is today."

"I met Howard one day," he says, "and told him that we would have to stop work on the project because we were running out of money, and he said, 'don't stop, Bill.' And he sent me his personal check for $20,000. I was also able to borrow some money from Lamar Life Insurance Company.

"And Harry Moir of Pure Oil (which is now Union Oil and still the sole supplier of gasoline at the Speedway) even gave me a $35,000 credit line on fuel used in the machinery for the construction. Paul Whiteman and Don Kendall and Harley Earl also went to bat for me. Harley was a vice president at GM in charge of styling at the time and he got us use of the corporate computers to help in designing the track's curve counters. Harley always said that the only way I got the whole thing completed, was that I was too dumb to know it couldn't be done."

There is more to the Speedway story.

When France entered into the contract with the legislatively created Recreational District the prime lessee of the land the Speedway is constructed on, the contract called for the District to hold the corporation harmless from taxes on the leased property because the property is owned by the city or county and all of the improvements someday revert to the county.

Several politicians in the State of Florida and even some of the members of the Florida Supreme Court ignore the Florida State Constitution which clearly spells out the "No law shall be passed which impairs a contract." The Speedway Corporation has been in various courts in Florida for about 15 years because the city, county and state officials are not living up to the con-

100

ditions of the contracts between the city of Daytona and the Racing District, or the authorities obligations to the Speedway Corporation.

France's experience with agreements with public officials in Florida has not been satisfactory in regards to those officials living up to their commitments.

France says that the Speedway Corporation pays well over a million dollars a year in taxes that he says are legally imposed. The tax in question is the $154,000 that is being charged in violation of the Agreements which the State and County are reneging on. Had the Speedway Corporation not lived up to its Agreement the County or City could have ousted them in 60 days.

During this period, the international sanctioning connection in the United States went belly-up.

"After the Vukovich accident at Indianapolis (1955 when two-time 500 winner Bill Vukovich was killed), the AAA decided to get out of racing," says France. "They wanted to divorce themselves from motorsports activities.

"I got in touch with Hubert Schroeder, then Secretary of the FIA (Federation Internationale de l'Automobile—the international racing governing body) and asked them to send a delegation to the United States. It was two years before ACCUS (the Automobile Competition Committee of the United States) was formed, but it was through my efforts, and it opened the door so NASCAR drivers can run in any listed national event. Or international. In fact, we were instrumental in getting Fireball Roberts to run at LeMans.

"The accomplishment of getting ACCUS started was one of the most important things that happened during our early years because it got NASCAR worldwide recognition," France points out.

There was irony connected with the move. A few years earlier France had gone to the Indianapolis 500 as the guest of a friend, and was kicked out—by the contest board of AAA.

"It was an unfortunate thing," France recalls. "It certainly wasn't Tony Hulman (then Speedway president). He and I were friends. It was the old contest board and they were jealous of NASCAR.

"I had been invited by a fellow who contributed a lap prize. Lap prize contributors received a badge for themselves that got them in the pits and the garage area, and one for a guest. I was his guest. But apparently somebody told a guy Bill France was in the pits. He asked a gateman to come over and tell me to get out.

"We (Bill and Annie) left and went back to Florida and built our own track," France chuckles.

Did that indignity give France any more incentive to complete the Daytona International Speedway?

"Well, it didn't hold us back any," France says with a wry smile.

But those who know Bill France, know that he would have completed the Speedway in spite of any odds. In fact, he did complete it with almost overwhelming odds against him, and the track that a few years before the *Indianapolis Star* had labeled a 'pipe dream' was, at last, a reality.

Here is how Jim Foster's Daytona public relations people—pros like Ron Meade and Jim Freeman—describe the facility:

Daytona International Speedway, the creation of William Henry Getty (Bill) France, is one of the most famous sports facilities in the world and is annually the scene of some of the greatest motor racing events.

The spacious multi-motorsports facility was constructed at an initial cost of more than $3 million. After years of promoting races on the old 4.1 mile beach/road course, Bill France staged the first Daytona 500 in February, 1959.

The excitement of the first 500-mile race, guaranteed the success of the Speedway and the Daytona 500.

Since the beginning, close competition with as many as 60 lead changes in a 200-lap, 500-mile race and average speeds of more than 190 miles per hour have thrilled thousands of fans during the 18 seasons the Speedway has been in operation. France, who serves as the President of International Speedway Corporation, saw a record crowd of more than 130,000 spectators for the 1977 Daytona 500.

Daytona International Speedway was built on a 455 acre tract and designed so the huge 2.5-mile trioval could be used for all types of motor racing. A twisting infield road course that is also linked with the Speedway proper is ideal for road racing. Altogether, there are five courses, the 2.5-mile trioval and road courses of 3.84, 3.87, 3.1 and 1.3 miles in length. The 3.87-mile course has a 100-yard chicane for the motorcycle road races on the long back straight of the trioval.

The east and west turns with 1,000 foot radii are banked 31 degrees, and a 2,000 foot pit access road extends along the north side of the track, just off the 18-degree banked turn on the front stretch.

Along the north side of the track are nine permanent grandstands which will accommodate more than 70,000 spectators. The stands are named after auto racing greats of the past.

The huge infield will accommodate 75,000 spectators and cars and it's also the site of many permanent buildings of accessory firms and other automotive oriented companies. The Speedway has it own security bureau, maintenance staff, fire department, ambulance corps and a first-rate, eight-bed care center which is completely staffed during the races.

Several modern buildings outside the Speedway proper house the corporation's general offices and the home office of NASCAR.

The mammoth racing plant was constructed with every consideration of the spectator in mind and the entire trioval plus the infield course may be viewed in entirety from any seat in the grandstands.

Five outlets across the track, in addition to the duel 250-foot tunnels in the northeast corner, make for rapid entrance and exit. An enormous information tower and scoreboard, operated by electronic equipment, rises out of the paddock or garage area. Officials atop the Campbell grandstands keep in touch via a complex telephone network, with every strategic point on the course. Two-way radio communication is also used.

A 160-seat, ultra modern press box for the working press, and posh lounges for dignitaries and VIPs are also in the grandstand area.

More than one million cubic yards of dirt were removed from the infield to build the high-banked turns, creating a man-made lake...Lake Lloyd...of 44 acres.

The mammoth Speedway is used for racing or testing more than 65 per cent of the year, and in the short time since Bill France first opened the gates in 1959, it has become the hub of racing in the United States and the world center of motor sport.

There was some concern as Speed Weeks drew near in 1959; concern for the weather and for the crowd as the sprawling racing plant sat empty, awaiting fans to cheer the beach racers on the two and one half miles of asphalt. There is always that concern among race promoters.

The weather forecast had called for rain for an extended period, and Bill France, better than anybody, knew that rain on the day of his first 500 mile race could spell financial ruin. But one old-timer, standing in line as the track opened, sucking on his pipe, summed up the feeling of confidence fans had everywhere. "Ain't gonna' rain on Sunday. France gonna' see to that," he said.

It didn't rain, and fans poured in from all over the Southeast. The sandy parking lots steadily filled as the people came for the week-long activity. But before most of them arrived, tragedy had struck the speedway. One of the early beach stars and hero of the Hudson days, Marshall Teague, was

Here's an aerial view of Daytona International Speedway as it looked on the day of the 1970 Daytona 500 NASCAR-FIA late model stock car classic.

driving Chapman Root's Indianapolis car, the Sumar Special, in special practice runs around the new speedway. The car had looked good the first couple of times around the tri-oval, but suddenly as it went into the second turn at 160 miles per hour, it lurched into a broad slide and began to flip. It spewed parts all over the course as it spun dizzily five times in mid air, landing 500 yards from the point where it started the slide. The seat, with Teague still in it, tore loose while the car was still flipping and landed 150 feet ahead of the chassis. Teague was found harnessed to the seat. Daytona's great local hero had been killed instantly.

As the late model stock cars arrived, they seemed to form a sort of memorial to Teague, who had been with them from the beginning. And these cars were just the sensation the fans had expected on the high banks. It was obvious that Bill France had again made the right move.

Along with the seasoned veterans of beach and dirt track racing and Darlington, came a rookie that was to make the most profound impression on stock car racing of anybody in history, Richard Petty. Richard had raced one season in the convertible class, but this was to be his inaugural year in the Grand National circuit. It would, if effect, pit Petty against Petty. Lee versus Richard.

It didn't take long for the cars to roar past the beach course records. Cotton Owens, in a 1958 Pontiac, turned in the fastest 500 qualifying time of 143.198; astounding, considering that this was his average all the way around the two and one half mile tri-oval. The record for the beach had been set by Paul Goldsmith the year before, also in a 1958 Pontiac. He had been clocked at 140.570, but that had been in a straightaway run with no turns.

Shorty Rollins in a Ford won the first stock car race at the new Daytona International Speedway, a 100-mile qualifying race. And Bob Welborn in a Chevrolet won the second 100-miler.

The stage was set for the inaugural Daytona 500.

If Bill France had been able to write a script for the race, it could not have been any more exciting.

Fifty-nine gleaming cars roared away as the starter dropped the green flag. Welborn, Tom Pistone and Little Joe Weatherly battled back and forth for the lead 22 laps. Fireball Roberts took over for the next 20 laps and from then on it was a series of lead changes and excitement that kept the crowd on its feet for most of the race.

Lee Petty in his Olds 88 took the lead at the 375-mile mark and five laps

Press corps has temporary area to cover first Daytona 500.

Charles Moneypenny, designer of Daytona International Speedway, gives the green flag to the first car to attempt speed trials in 1959 when the track opened. Bill France, Sr., center, checks his watch while John Bruner, Sr., official NASCAR starter, is at right.

Capacity crowd was treated to some close, high-speed action, never seen before in the South.

The infield was jammed as inaugural race drew a larger crowd than expected.

The history-making finish of the first Daytona 500, with the late Joe Weatherly unlapping himself in the top car, a Chevrolet; Lee Petty in the center in a Plymouth; and Johnny Beauchamp in bottom lane in a Thunderbird. Beauchamp was first declared the winner but this was changed to Petty three days later after all photographs were studied.

Bill France, Sr., left, presents the 1959 Daytona 500 trophy to Lee Petty in the garage area, three days after the historic event when it was finally determined, from photographs, he was the winner.

Lee Petty, with car, prior to Daytona 500 in 1959.

later Johnny Beauchamp eased past in his Ford Thunderbird. After that it was a seesaw battle for the rest of the race, with Petty leading one lap and Beauchamp the next. On the last lap, Petty, Beauchamp and Weatherly (who was one lap down) roared down the tri-oval in front of the grandstands three abreast. They ran wheel to wheel through the high-banks of the west turn and down the back straightaway. The three cars roared through turns three and four as if they were welded together, not one of them giving an inch.

The three thundered across the finish line in what appeared to be a dead heat. At first Beauchamp was thought to be the winner. And then Petty. But there was no use, they would have to rely on the photograph of the finish. It took three days of studying the photograph before the NASCAR panel finally declared Lee Petty the winner of the first Daytona 500. Richard had finished a disappointing 57th but his career in Grand National racing was underway. And it was to be one that nobody would ever forget—and maybe never match.

Richard's impressions of the new speedway seemed to echo those of the other drivers, but, being a rookie, his were perhaps a little more objective. He had this to say;

"I had just as much chance in this one as anybody; in fact, being a rookie might have given me a slight edge. *Nobody* knew anything about driving in this big oval, so we were starting even—just as Daddy had in the first Grand National race at Charlotte. But my *edge* was due to the fact that I didn't have to *unlearn* any short track habits. The others had formed well-learned patterns, and at Daytona they were having to do things differently. The track was giving some of them a fit. For once, not knowing anything was a blessing. It was *all* new to me, so if they decided to run on the inside of the track, and I decided I could go better on the outside, my guess was as good as theirs. In fact, most drivers ran as they did on the other tracks, where the groove was on the inside; it wasn't there at Daytona.

"I just went out there and said 'here's a big old track with plenty of room. I believe I'll run up here.' And I did. I formed a habit of running up high because I didn't have much horsepower. I *had* to run up near the fence and then come charging off the banks to keep the engine wound up. This was the only way I could remain competitive, just run wide open all the way around the track and use the high banks to my advantage.

"I found out it lets the car run on its own merit," Richard says, "It sort of frees it up, and it's a whole bunch easier on the car and the tires—and the driver—than it is when you just go down and turn left, that's what bogs the car down. But if you go down in the corner and turn it easier (like coming off the banks), the rolling friction doesn't slow the car down as much."

Petty also discovered another interesting phenomenon in that first qualifying race, although it took him—and the other drivers, who must have experienced the same thing—a while to realize what it was.

"I first noticed the effect when I was running off the banks to keep up with the pack," Petty says. "'Every once in a while I would go whizzing right by them as if they had stopped, and then, a little later, they would come flying by me—the whole pack I had just blown off. I said 'Man, there's something going on here.' I didn't know what it was, but I began experimenting and found a place where my car was running faster than anybody's—a spot where I could get by.

"I would follow the pack close through the corner. Then, when we came out of the turn, I would pull out and go flying by them. The race strategy became clear all of a sudden when I got up to fourth place with five laps to go. I decided just to wait there until the last lap and zing past them for the checkered flag. I hung back until we got the white flag, meaning one lap to go, and then I jockeyed into position. Everybody went into the first corner real low, I went high and came off the second corner—the spot where

Drafting—Richard Petty, at right, shoves his bumper into contact with Buddy Baker's Dodge, at left, in typical drafting maneuver to gain speed.

I found I could pick up speed—with a sling-shot effect. I was actually catching their draft but didn't know it. The car shot around them into first place.

"That car was really moving," says Petty, "right down the back straight, and I thought, 'Man, this is going to be easy.' But when we got to the third corner, the other cars went by me like I wasn't there. I had done the right thing, all right, I had just done it too soon; they caught *my* draft coming off two.

"I was a little puzzled as to what this new sensation on the Daytona track was, so I didn't say a word to anybody, not even Daddy. But I watched him from the pits in the 500 mile race—after I had gone out. He was running the Olds, and Johnny Beauchamp, running in a Thunderbird, was battling him for first place. On one lap I would see Daddy go right by him, and I couldn't understand why he didn't keep right on going. Then Joe Weatherly, in the Chevrolet, would go right past the two of them, and then *he* seemed to slow down. This went on all afternoon, and everybody in the stands were going right out of their minds. The three of them had discovered 'drafting' on their own without being told by some rookie," Petty chuckled.

The crowd must have loved the whole show, because they all returned on July 4 for the first Firecracker 250. And the drivers returned to put on a show. But it was a different kind of show. This one all belonged to Fireball Roberts and his Pontiac.

"The 250 was Fireball's kind of race," says Jim Hunter, Talladega P.R. chief, "The kind he could win. Fireball always seemed to run his equipment harder then anybody else's, and in the sprint type races, man, he was hard to beat."

Fireball qualified on the pole and just stayed out front most of the race to win, although Weatherly in a Thunderbird convertible (they mixed the two classes) was running in the same lap at the finish. Fireball's *race* average of 140.581 miles per hour was slightly faster than the quickest straightaway beach qualifying run.

Fireball, as usual, was sanguine about his accomplishment. In an interview with veteran reporter, Benny Kahn, he said:

People seem to think race drivers have special courage, it's not so. It doesn't take any more guts to be a race driver than it does to a be jet pilot or a steeplejack or a lot of things. There's a lot of difference between having guts in racing and being plain foolish. Guts is experience. You learn the hard way what you can do in a car and to a car. You know how much punishment the car can stand and how much you can stand and how you react.

Doing something you have no idea that you can do or that the car can do is plain stupid. It takes good thinking to win a race, preparation by expert mechanics and a good ride by the driver, and even if you get all that together just right, you aren't going to see that checkered flag wave for you unless Lady Luck smiles a lot on your side.

He was to see the checkered flag wave for him three times in the Firecracker, each time in a Smokey Yunick-prepared Pontiac.

"Fireball was one of the few who fared better in the switch to the speedway," says Bill Tuthill. "There were some who didn't make the switch all that well. And there was Herb Thomas, who had gotten hurt on a half-mile track and never even tried the speedway, and that's a shame because he was so good. Maybe the best. But Fireball never had done all that well on the beach. He tried to be like Curtis (Turner), but he wound up upside down a lot. Fireball was superb on the speedway, though. It was a thrill to watch him.

"And it sure was nice to go to a race at the new track. There were nice seats and you could set a race a year in advance. You didn't have to check with Washington for tide charts or any of that. And there were a *lot* of drivers from the beach days to watch at the speedway," Tuthill says. "Lee and Buck (Baker) made the switch with no problems, and Joe Weatherly and Curtis and Junior Johnson. Although Buck always disliked super speedway racing."

"I think competition actually got tougher, when we moved to the speedway," says France. "For one thing, it doubled attendance and gave us more prize money, and this got more attention. I guess it expanded the public's awareness of Daytona. I know it got more manufacturers interested, like Goodyear, for instance.

"The interstate system was just getting started then, and the strains that were being put on tires—and cars, for that matter—were much greater. Driving at 75 or 80 miles an hour all day long on a hot day was something that could be related to the speedway, so both Goodyear and Firestone needed it to improve their products. It's one of the benefits the public was to get from racing. And the durability of the car and transmissions and rear ends and everything improved because of the information they were getting at our high speeds for 500 miles," he says proudly.

1961 Ford being tested in summer of 1960. L to r: Joe Epton, NASCAR; Darel Dieringer; Glen Wood; Leonard Wood; Curtis Turner and Dick Dolan.

Richard Petty, 43, in qualifying run for the 500 in 1960.

Bud Moore slides past Mario Andretti in the 1960 five hundred mile race.

Junior Johnson, 27, on his way to victory, passes Curtis Turner in the 1960 five hundred.

Sixty-eight cars started the 1960 Daytona 500, which must have sounded like an earthquake to the few people of Volusia County who weren't at the track. Fireball Roberts had qualified at 151.556 miles per hour, which, much to France's delight, was to be faster than the pole-sitter that year at the Indianapolis 500. Roberts got off to an early lead, but, along with Indianapolis great Parnelli Jones, he went out early.

Most of the afternoon the Rhonda, North Carolina, chicken farmer, Junior Johnson, was out front in his 1959 Chevrolet. Johnson, who had come out of the hills with as much experience racing with revenuers as on the race track, was challenged often by Lee Petty and Bobby Johns, and even *Richard* Petty, who led the race for 28 laps. But in the end, Johnson's Chevy blazed to victory, with Johns second and Richard placing third, one spot in front of his daddy.

The purse for the race made Johnson $19,600 richer, quite a contrast to the $350 France had won 20 years earlier on the beach.

Veteran Jack Smith in a Pontiac continued the General Motors domination in the Firecracker 250 that year as he streaked home just in front of Cotton Owens. One lap behind them was newcomer Fred Lorenzen in a Ford. Out of contention due to mechanical difficulties was another new name, David Pearson.

1960 Firecracker winner Jack Smith won 21 Grand National races during his career.

M. F. Thomas, left, of Corona Del Mar, California, holds his trophies, but his chief interest is the check which Bill France, Sr., president of NASCAR is holding. Thomas, driving a 125 hp Rambler American six-cylinder took top honors in the 1960 Pure Oil Economy Trials at the Daytona International Speedway. Thomas drove his Rambler 51.281 miles on one gallon of gas—nearly seven miles farther than his nearest opponent.

The 1961 Daytona 500 was to be one of the major stumbling blocks for the Pettys in their racing history. It all began in the first qualifying race. On the last lap, Fireball came by in the lead, with Junior right behind him in a draft. Richard had just tagged onto the draft when Junior hit an object on the track, blowing the right front tire. His car spun to the right, and Richard dove to the left to avoid hitting him. Junior crashed against the wall and bounced back toward Richard, who had spun onto the track apron. As Petty reached the grass, Junior's car caught up with him and hit him in the right rear quarter panel, sending the Petty car directly back across the track. When it got to the guard rail, it sort of lifted up and went sailing over and far below into the parking lot, a drop of about four stories.

"I could feel the concrete ripping everything out from under the car as I went over," says Petty. "And then, suddenly, the car was off the wall, and sailing through the air. When I hit, I can remember seeing all the body panels twisting and tearing. And then it stopped. I crawled out falling to the ground, and sat there, and just looked at the car. It was completely totaled, but I kept hearing this familiar noise," he says. "then I figured it out—the engine was still running. Well, I limped back over—I limped because I had sprained my ankle gettin' out of the car. Ain't that sumptin'—and I was

The remains of the Johnny Beauchamp car, left, and the Lee Petty car after they both crashed during one of the qualifying races for the 1961 500.

1961 Firecracker winner David Pearson leads in car No. 3, followed by Bobby Johns, 72, Nelson Stacy, 29, Fred Lorenzen, 28, and Larry Frank, 76.

leaning inside, turning the motor off when the ambulance arrived.

"Those cats thought I had been thrown half out of the car and they loaded me right in and took me to the track hospital. They wouldn't listen. And when I got to the hospital, the doctor rushed over and said, 'where are you hurt, Richard? Do you know what it was that hurt you?' I said, 'Yeah, I fell out of my car.'

"He looked at me like I musta' been knocked out of my head and he said, 'you mean you were *thrown* out of your car.' And I said, 'no, I *fell* out after the wreck.' "

By the time Richard got out of the hospital, the second qualifying race had reached the last lap. He heard the announcer on the loud-speaker saying 'they've just dropped the white flag and the leaders are going into the first turn.'

"I thought, 'it's just exactly where and when it happened to me in the first race,' when I heard the crash, and I looked up and I could see Daddy's car sailing up through the air and over the wall, with Johnny Beauchamp's car fused right into the rear end of it. There was silence for a second and the big crash."

Lee had been following Banjo Matthews, who got sideways in the turn, and he backed off, getting sideways himself. Beauchamp, who was roaring up on the pair, hit Lee in the rear, wide open, driving both Petty's car and his, with the bumpers hooked together, through the fence at 150 miles an hour.

It was the final race for Lee Petty, the three-time NASCAR champion, who was injured so badly that he still walks with a limp.

Pole-sitter Fireball Roberts led most of the 500 that year, but exited the race with 13 laps to go, leaving the wreck-strewn event to Marvin Panch in another Pontiac.

The Firecracker that year looked again as if it was to be Fireball's day. He started on the pole and was followed into the first turn by the 1960 rookie of the year, David Pearson, driving a Ray Fox-prepared Pontiac. It took Pearson 42 laps to catch Fireball, and then he only held the lead for three laps, but he remained in contention. When Freddy Lorenzen took over from Roberts on Lap 81 of the 100-lapper, Pearson moved right into the draft with the leaders, and stayed there. Fireball began to fade and a lengthy pit stop took him out of contention, but Pearson stayed right on Lorenzen's bumper and passed the Elmhurst, Illinois, flash in the last lap to win the 1961 Firecracker 250.

Bill France, Sr., and David Pearson in Victory Circle after Pearson won the 1961 Daytona Firecracker 250.

The great success at Daytona had prompted the building of new superspeedways at Atlanta and Charlotte, and Pearson dominated the sport in 1961—his second season in Grand National racing—winning three races that year on the super tracks, causing Jim Foster, who was then sports editor of the *Spartanburg Herald*, to label him "Little David, the Giant Killer."

Pearson came close to winning a fourth superspeedway race that year, the Atlanta 500, when he chased Roberts and Weatherly into a turn. He didn't back off one bit when he caught them, and the three entered the turn, side by side. All three of them hit the wall. There are still some who think the then-popular Jim Reeves' song "Hello Wall" was dedicated to Pearson because of the Atlanta crash.

But Pearson had risen rapidly. Joe Whitlock, who directs public relations for Humpy Wheeler at the Charlotte Motor Speedway, had this to say about Pearson:

"David Pearson is the epitome of a national champion. His ability to negotiate the dirt tracks of the Carolinas in a sportsman racer was almost legendary and he ended his illustrious sportsman career in 1959, a year that saw him win 30 of the 42 races he entered and walk away with the South Carolina championship.

"Pearson entered Grand National competition in 1960 and promptly won the Rookie of the Year honors for his efforts. The following season he won events at Daytona, Atlanta and Charlotte. He scored the first 'grand slam' in the history of the sport when he won the Rebel 400 at Darlington. Who else but Pearson would have been the first to take victories at all of the South's major speedways?"

The building of the Charlotte Motor Speedway was to be a particularly vexing problem for Bill France. His old racing buddy, Curtis Turner—the man with whom he had shared the thrills of the Mexican Road Race and the old beach course days, was building the track and, early in the game, had run low on funds.

In an effort to keep the project going, Turner had gone to the Teamsters to get a loan, and they agreed to help finance the new superspeedway, reportedly providing that Turner would help them organize the Grand National drivers. It was the biggest problem that France had faced since the Glenn Dunnaway case following the 1949 Charlotte race.

France reacted strongly to the threat of unionized race drivers. He suspended Turner, and this destroyed any hopes the Teamsters had of getting a foot in the NASCAR door. But the fans reacted to the loss of one of their favorite drivers. Curtis Turner, and his wham-bam driving style, was the idol of many, and they carried signs to races for a while, protesting his suspension. But, fortunately for France, it came at a time when his new crop of super stars was on the rise. Richard Petty and David Pearson and Buck Baker's son, Buddy, had joined the ever-popular Junior Johnson and Fireball Roberts and Marvin Panch in the thundering charges to the finish lines of Grand National racing, and the fans soon forgot about the Turner suspension. There was just too much action out there on the track to worry about the politics of a single driver, even one of the stature of Curtis Turner.

Pontiac and Fireball Roberts continued their domination of the Daytona track in 1962, and a few fans suggested changing the name of the track to the "Fireball International Speedway."

The colorful Daytona resident started from the pole in the 500 and battled for the first 66 laps with Junior Johnson, also in a Pontiac. After Johnson went out of the race, there was little competition, except from Richard Petty, who was making the draft work for him. Petty was nearly eight miles an hour slower than Roberts, but by latching on to the speedy Number 22 Pontiac, he was able to stay in second place most of the afternoon, and actually led a few times when Roberts pitted. Petty was able to hold on for a second place finish.

Pontiac was up to 421 cubic inches in their powerful V-8, with an estimated 465 horsepower and was clearly the leader in performance—but the others had begun to build toward the biggest engine war in NASCAR history. Ford increased their displacement to 406 and Mopar countered by offering their 413-inch engine for both Dodge and Plymouth. Chevy upped their 348 engine to 409.

The difference in horsepower was apparent on the high banks and the long straights. The Fords just couldn't last. Most of them left the race with blown engines, resulting from cracked blocks.

The best finish Ford could manage in the Firecracker 250 in 1962 was a third place by Marvin Panch. Up front again it was Fireball Roberts, giving him a clean sweep of the Daytona races that year (he had even won the qualifying race he was in).

Joe Weatherly, left, 1962 NASCAR champion, and Rene Dentan, president of Rolex Watch U.S.A., synchronize their Rolex watches in anticipation of the 1963 Daytona 500. Rolex is the official timepiece of the Daytona International Speedway.

Cotton Owens, right, chats with David Pearson prior to 1962 qualifying. The Spartanburg mechanic got Pearson off to a good start.

Fireball had taken home more than $40,000 from Daytona alone in 1962. The sport of stock car racing, Southern-style, had definitely been lifted from the days of meager purses and shabby equipment. The factories were lining up solidly behind their cars, and they readied for battle as the 1963 season opened.

"The money," Fireball said, "has affected all of us. It has generally upgraded everything—even the people you associate with are higher, socially. Of course, we all started from the bottom, so we don't have any place else to go."

"The sport and the drivers have matured with age," Bill France said. "The drivers in those early years of NASCAR—the Flocks, Byron, Thomas and the others—could compete equally with the guys of today, if they were using the same equipment. But today's driver has more things working for him. His contacts with the manufacturers, the great acceptance of the sport by the public, the superspeedways, the recognition of the media, the tremendous cars. All of these things have placed today's racing competitor on a par with the competitor in our other major sports."

Ford and Chrysler announced plans for full participation in stock car racing in 1963. Ford corrected their block-cracking problem by cross-bolting the main bearings, and the maneuver paid off. And the 500 that year was to have a dramatic beginning and end.

Marvin Panch had been thought to have the best chance of any Ford driver in the 500, but Johnny Rutherford had put a Chevrolet on the pole, so the Ford hopes were still not all that high. They were deflated even more when Panch crashed a Ferrari in practice for the 24-hour sports car race on Daytona's road course. The car burst into flames and Panch was trapped inside, but fellow-stock car driver Tiny Lund, a 265 pound giant, ran to his aid and helped pull him from the burning racer. Panch was seriously burned and obviously would not be able to drive in the 500, so, from his hospital bed, he asked car-owner Glenn Wood to replace him with Lund.

Junior Johnson, in a Chevrolet, took an early lead and intended to run away from the pack, but Pontiac pilot Paul Goldsmith jumped onto Junior's draft and the two cars sped around the track all by themselves for the first 26 laps. Neither lasted. Johnson went out with mechanical problems on the 26th lap and Goldsmith exited on the 39th. The Fords that had been chasing them had already started to move up. And another Daytona phenomenon was unfolding—the Wood brothers pit work. Each pit stop that Lund made moved him a little closer to the front—and the Fords continued to look better.

"All the Fords run better when there are other cars on the track," said

Racing is not always serious, as Tiny Lund proves by carrying Marty Robbins to his car.

From left, Marvin Panch, Glen Wood, Leonard Wood and Freddy Lorenzen discuss track conditions following qualifying.

Glenn Wood. "It doesn't seem like they go as well in qualifying, but when the air gets stirred up and going in the same direction, the Fords go about as strong as anything out here."

It proved to be true.

By the 175-mile mark, Bobby Johns was the only driver left in contention with a General Motors car. A.J. Foyt, in a Pontiac, and G.C. Spencer, in a Chevrolet, had led briefly, but they were gone. And when Johns ran out of fuel, it left the battle completely to the Fords.

The fight was between Freddy Lorenzen and Ned Jarrett, with Lund—who had never won a Grand National race—right behind them. The Wood brothers had Lund on a strict schedule. He was to draft the leaders and come in for fuel every 100 miles. With this plan, and the fantastic pit action, Lund would be ready to make his move later in the race. And make a move he did. When he pitted the last time, with 40 laps to go, it was wild action. Lund beat Lorenzen by a full ten seconds and Jarrett by six as the three Fords roared into and out of the pits.

Lund was getting better mileage on his gasoline than either of the two cars because he had been conserving his fuel in the draft, so when Lorenzen had to pit again with only seven laps to go, Jarrett and Lund roared by. Jarrett realized exactly what the situation was and he dropped behind Lund to conserve his own fuel and try to avoid another pit stop that would cost him the race. It was not a battle for speed at this point—because the two were well ahead of the rest of the field—but one of fuel economy.

Three laps later, Jarrett realized he couldn't make it, so he headed for the pits, leaving Lund in front. With Jarrett out, Lund cut his speed and

From left, Joe Weatherly, Earl Kelly, Bob Colvin and Ned Jarrett, pose in front of the Southern 500 trophy.

NASCAR great Ned Jarrett and a quartet of fast machines.

A familiar sight in early NASCAR days, Junior Johnson in the winner's circle.

prayed. It was going to be very close, but he had no choice, he had to stay out there and try to finish the last two laps with the fuel he had. Lorenzen was back on the track with plenty of gas and flying, trying to catch the slowing Lund. Lund's car started missing in the turns as the little gasoline left sloshed around in the tank. The engine would die in the turns and catch again on the straights. Finally there was one lap to go. The engine coughed in one and two and three and quit completely coming out of the fourth turn. Lund was coasting toward the finish line as Lorenzen roared into the third turn. Jarrett was flying out of two.

Lund's engine caught one more time as he glided down the tri-oval and sputtered to a stop as he crossed the finish line to take the checkered flag 24 seconds ahead of Lorenzen and 30 seconds in front of Jarrett.

Chevrolet announced their withdrawal of factory participation following the race and Ford ran hugh newspaper ads all over the country, proclaiming "Ford Sweeps Daytona." They had taken the first five places, ending a General Motors domination that had persisted since the track opened. It was the height of Ford factory sponsorship as they adopted the "Total Performance" theme.

Ford's total domination of the sport became even more apparent when they lured away GM's top driver, Fireball Roberts.

The Golden Boy of 60s Grand National racing, Freddy Lorenzen, was one of Ford's stalwarts.

Cale Yarborough experiences some major engine problems during the 1963 Modified-Sportsman race.

Junior Johnson escaped with a cut on the forehead in the crash of his Pontiac in a 1964 qualifying race.

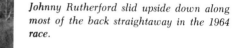

Johnny Rutherford slid upside down along most of the back straightaway in the 1964 race.

Bay Darnell became one of the first to put a car into Lake Lloyd, inside the tri-oval at the speedway.

Dieringer put his Mercury on the pole. It was the only lead Dearborn had. Petty got to the corner first and led the initial 39 laps. Earl Balmer led one lap while Richard pitted and the rest of the day it was either Petty, Bobby Isaac or Foyt. At about the half-way point Petty blew his engine and left the battle to Isaac and Foyt, who switched back and forth almost every lap.

On the last lap, Foyt in the Ray Nichels Dodge, came out of turn two and roared down off the bank, forcing Isaac down low. There had been but two choices for Isaac: hit Foyt or back off so the Catawba, North Carolina, driver went for the apron and slowed down to avoid spinning, giving Foyt a clear shot at the victory. It was a six-car Mopar sweep.

Another blow had come to Ford at Charlotte in the World 600, and it was one that was felt throughout the entire racing world. On the seventh lap of the race, Junior Johnson spun coming out of two, sliding right into the path of Ned Jarrett and Fireball Roberts. The crash that followed sent Fireball's car smashing into an abutment along the inner wall, driving the gas tank up into the driver's compartment. The car exploded and Fireball was trapped. Jarrett ran to his aid and helped pull him out, but Fireball was burned over 75 percent of his body.

Six weeks later—just two days before the 1964 Firecracker, the race that belonged to him—Glenn "Fireball" Roberts died. Stock car racing had lost it's all-time favorite.

Fireball had entered the world of stock car racing in a time of fierce competition for small purses, when winning first place was the only thing that counted. It was the heyday of the hard-chargers. When the flag dropped, there was always the mad charge for the front. To stay alive in that kind of action, a driver had to develop a racing skill of the highest order. Fireball's career bore the stamp of those lessons, and he had but one style—get out front and stay there.

In the annals of auto racing at Daytona, there has never been a feat to match that of Fireball Roberts in the Smokey Yunick Number 22 Pontiac. Imagine, if you can, one driver in one car making a clean sweep of every event in which he competed for the entire season of 1962 at the Daytona International Speedway.

Not only did Fireball score a grand slam but he streaked to a new record speed, regardless of the distance, every time out. Six record-breaking victories, extending from the early February time trials to the drop of the checkered flag on July 4th. And, in winning the 500, he carved his name in auto racing history as the first man ever to win a 500-mile race at a speed over 150 miles an hour.

Race driver Richard Petty pauses during Goodyear tire tests at the Daytona International Speedway to examine four tires that were purposely slashed and punctured at high speeds while he tested a new safety concept in racing tires. An inner tire which remained inflated assisted Petty in maintaining control of the car.

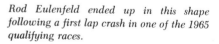

Rod Eulenfeld ended up in this shape following a first lap crash in one of the 1965 qualifying races.

The infighting between Ford and Chrysler had started long before the 1964 season ended. Ford demanded of France that the overhead cam engine be allowed for 1965, Mopar insisted that everything remain the same. So France called officials of the two companies together and, after several days of haggling, it was apparent that there was not going to be any amicable solution to the factory battle.

If France allowed the overhead cam engine of Ford, Chrysler would go back to the drawing board and come up with an even more exotic power plant than their Hemi. And all of racing would be even further from the "stock" engine configuration. After all, France reasoned, there must be a certain number of the engines available to the general motoring public before they can be legal for racing.

Ford, meanwhile, said they would not compete in 1965 if the rules remained the same. Chrysler countered by saying they wouldn't compete if the rules were changed to allow the new Ford engine.

France met again with industry officials, this time in Detroit, but the outcome was the same. Ford said they must have the single overhead cam engine, Chrysler said that if Ford got that, then they would come out with the same thing, except that theirs would be a *double* overhead cam version.

The meetings and hassle that followed for the next few months were unprecedented. The result was that France banned the Hemi in the small Belvidere model because it was not available to the public in that model, and Chrysler pulled out of NASCAR racing. The rules had stated that engine displacement remained the same at 428 cubic inches, but that the Chrysler dual carbs and Ford's dual high-rise intake manifold were out. The Hemi engine was never banned in the fury model, but Chrysler wanted to race the narrower Belvidere.

Chrysler Vice President Bob Anderson said "Racing has always prided itself on being progressive, and here we are now, backing up."

At Ford, Leo Bebee, head of special vehicles, said "NASCAR is to be congratulated for its efforts to speed progress."

Two unusual and diametrically opposed definitions of "progress."

The outcome in 1965 was predictable. Ford ran away with everything and track promoters screamed. But Bill France held his ground, knowing full well that, regardless of what one manufacturer or another said, they would be back.

As if France didn't have enough problems in 1965, rain shortened the 500 to 332-1/2 miles, leaving Lorenzen out in front of Dieringer and Bobby Johns. There was not a single non-Ford product in the top ten cars, and gone from the race entirely were such names as Richard Petty, David Pearson, Jimmy Pardue, Bobby Isaac, Jim Paschal, and Lee Roy Yarbrough. It was definitely a tainted Ford victory.

Fred Lorenzen, 28, charges through the pack to win the 1965 Daytona 500.

A.J. Foyt became a member of the Ford team and dominated the Firecracker in 1965. About the only excitement came late in the race when Foyt, who was so comfortably in front that his crew was lounging on the stacks of tires around his pits, came roaring into the pits and slid to a halt. His crew stumbled, fell and crawled to the wall. Ford's top executives, who sat in expensive seats across the way, leaped to their feet, because Buddy Baker was in second place, way back, but in second place. And in a Plymouth.

Foyt leaned out of the window and yelled to his crew: "Y'all want me for anything?" And he dumped the car into first and roared out of the pits and into the first turn, well ahead of Baker, who was just coming down the back straightaway. The comic move—although one that could have backfired if the car had stalled in the pits—left everybody with any Ford allegiance at all, near collapse.

Foyt went on to win handily.

The engine war was not over. Ford knew full well that Chrysler had produced enough Hemi engines for passenger cars in 1965 to make it eligible for the stock category under NASCAR rules, and would enable them to race it in 1966, so they announced that they would run the single overhead cam engine.

The new NASCAR rules were amended to read: "No overhead cam engines permitted unless approved by NASCAR. Volume production engines only (no limited production engines) and the volume production classification will be determined by spot checks at the various assembly lines when such checks are deemed necessary."

When the Ford engine was ruled "non-production," Bebee announced withdrawal for Ford. It meant that Chrysler would be back, but Ford would be gone. Not much of an improvement over the 1965 situation. But France worked out a compromise with Ford. NASCAR agreed to reconsider its decision once Ford had met production status with the engine.

A smiling Richard Petty holds the victor's spoils after winning the 1966 Daytona 500.

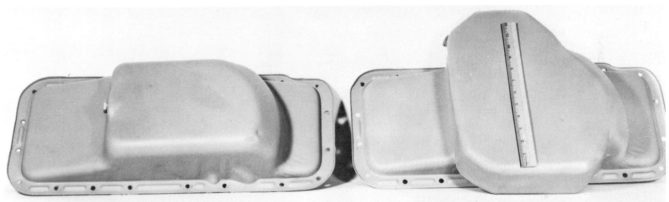

One of the first steps in transforming a passenger car into a racer, is the removal of standard instrument cluster and replacing with direct reading gauges (top photo) to measure oil and water temperatures and pressures and amp output. A tach replaces the speedometer. Standard 4-qt. oil pan (above, left) is converted to 8-qt. racing pan (right) to insure adequate oil supply in high speed turns. 1½-qt.-capacity oil cooler (left) is mounted next to water radiator to keep engine oil temperatures between 180 and 260 degrees.

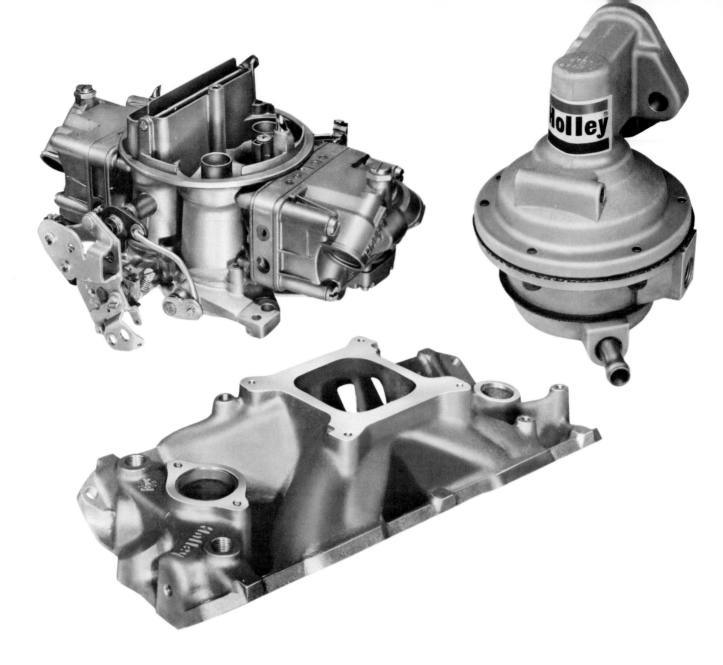

The first car at the track for practice for the '66 five hundred-miler was Petty's familiar blue Number 43. When someone asked Daddy Lee what they were doing there so early, Lee replied, "Early? We're a year behind now."

But it didn't take Richard long to catch up. He won the pole position and proceeded to set a pace of 170 miles per hour during the race. The pace was so torrid that tires began to throw chunks of rubber, which, like everything else during those days, found the Fords as their major targets. The windshields were destroyed on most of the leading Dearborn racers, including Marvin Panch, Dick Hutcherson and the old pro, Curtis Turner, who had been reinstated by France as a sort of appeasement to the fans.

But when everything had settled, Petty had won by a full lap. Cale Yarborough was second, David Pearson third, Freddy Lorenzen fourth, Sam McQuagg fifth and Jim Hurtubise sixth. Yarborough and Lorenzen were in two of the only Fords left.

The Firecracker 400 was another Mopar day, but this time it was newcomer Sam McQuagg who raced from fourth starting position into the first turn to take the lead that he relinquished only briefly during the entire

Sam McQuagg won the 1966 Firecracker in his Dodge.

afternoon. McQuagg went on to win the race, leading all but 32 laps.

Petty had challenged at one point but a blown engine on the 86th lap threw him into a collision with Earl Balmer. In the final analysis, the only Ford products in contention were Dieringer and Curtis Turner in second and fourth places.

It was a time of big spending—cubic dollars in many cases, instead of cubic inches. Ford and Chrysler were at it tooth and nail and Goodyear and Firestone were butting heads in the tire wars. Engine and chassis and body design changes were commonplace. It was a time when money seemed to be no object. Winning was everything.

"It seems like the drivers have grown up, but the manufacturers haven't," observed one long-time NASCAR follower.

"We didn't know the manufacturers would go to the extent they would to win," says France. "We've still got a bunch of their stuff stored out in a barn at the Speedway—aluminum hoods, bumpers, acid-dipped body panels—all of which was found out by the inspectors to be illegal."

And every race produced modifications that were ruled illegal. Everybody was caught up in the whirlwind of the change-or-run-second syndrome.

Speeds were going up and up. To help combat this, Goodyear went to Daytona with Darel Dieringer and Richard Petty to test an innovation that was so successful that it became manditory for NASCAR racers on superspeedways. They had redesigned their highway Double Eagle inner tire for the race track. It was a tire within a tire and said to be the greatest safety factor of anything in racing.

Joe Hawkes and his engineers placed sharp objects on the track and Dieringer and Petty actually ran over them at speeds up to 150 miles per hour, purposely blowing the outer tire to see if the inner casing would hold the car stable.

"Here we've spent all our lives trying to miss things on the track, and now we're out here trying to *hit* them," Dieringer said. "It sure keeps your attention."

The drivers and engineers, and particularly the Goodyear P.R. types, held their breath a lot in those days," says Bill Newkirk, Goodyear's public relations director.

The inner tire worked and France immediately announced that NASCAR had ruled them a must for tracks one mile and over in length. And then he went back to worrying about what the auto manufacturers had up their sleeves next.

An early NASCAR publicity photo featured orchestra leader Paul Whiteman in the foreground and Grand National cars on the beach. Whiteman was of great assistance to Bill France in building the speedway.

But NASCAR is not the only form of racing to come out of Daytona. No history of racing at Daytona would be complete without acknowledging the importance of motorcycles, IMSA and ARCA.

The fact that motorcycles have been passed over in this book does not mean they do not hold an important place in beach and speedway history. It means merely that they are a book in themselves. Their history, dating back to the first race in 1937, would fill as many pages as this automotive racing history. Anything less would be an injustice to the sport of motorcycle racing.

Early action in the 1967 Daytona 200.

Yvon DuHamel, 5, and Ron Gould, 27, in the 1969 Victory Lane for the 250cc race.

The start of the 1969 Expert race. Front row, left to right, Art Bauman, Mike Duff, Ron Gould, Yvon DuHamel, Ron Pierce.

The American Motorcycle Association's longest, richest and most prestigious bike race is held annually at Daytona International Speedway. This is the starting grid for the 1970 Daytona 200 AMA classic with Gene Romero (No. 3) on the pole with a record speed. Eventual winner was Dick Mann (second from left) aboard the No. 2 Honda.

Gene Romero, 3, leads Steve McLaughlin, 83, through a turn in the 1975 race.

Kenny Roberts, 2, and Johnny Cicotto, 5, in 1976 action in the Daytona 200.

Kenny Roberts' patented knee-blistering cornering technique.

Kawasaki team members, from left, Yvon DuHamel, Gary Nixon and Paul Smart.

Harley-Davidson great Jay Springsteen has been a Daytona favorite in recent years.

Yamaha star Steve Baker at Daytona in 1976.

Kurt Lentz heads for the hay bales in the 1978 Daytona 200.

Kenny Roberts leads the field in the 1978 Daytona 200.

Steve Baker pits in the 1978 Daytona 200.

The Automotive Racing Club of America (ARCA) became an instant tradition at Daytona with the 1964 running, and each February it is an important cog in the Speed Weeks program. A major stock car event.

Under the firm and positive direction of John Marcum, ARCA drivers from all over America compete annually in the thrilling spectacle that is second only to the Daytona 500, and often more exciting.

ARCA is in its 29th year of operation, and Marcum is sometimes referred to as the P.T. Barnum of automobile racing, clearly indicating the type of race show he has always put on.

Sports car racing, although not always as dramatic as stock cars, was a natural for the high banks and the infield course. The first sports car races in 1959 were run in a clockwise direction, a concession Bill France made to the European style of driving. But that lasted only one year, and in 1960 the sports cars ran in the same direction as their stock car counterparts.

Bill France got it started, but it was another man who spurred it on to great heights—orchestra leader Paul Whiteman.

To the sports car racer, Paul Whiteman was more than just the "King of Jazz." "Pop," as he was known among his friends from one end of the world to the other, was also a member of the board of directors at the Daytona International Speedway and served as director of sports car racing activities.

Whiteman, who died in 1967 at the age of 77, probably did more than any other man to develop a sports car racing program at Daytona. He was able to secure the speedway complex for the Sports Car Club of America (SCCA) national and regional races, and he also helped bring international endurance racing to Daytona in 1962, when the first three-hour Continental race was held.

His forceful, enthusiastic leadership was behind expansion of the Continental into one of the world's major racing events—the 24-Hours of Daytona.

"Pops" loved sports car racing, and this undoubtedly made the promoter's job much easier when it came to naming the speedway's annual August sports car races. So it was that in 1961 the first Paul Whiteman Trophy Races were held at Daytona.

Sportscars go the "wrong way" on the high banks at Daytona in 1959. In a concession to European style the cars raced clockwise during the first year of sports car racing at Daytona.

Carroll Shelby at Daytona in the early 60s.

The first winner was Bill Bencker of Jacksonville, Florida, who averaged 95.5 mph in an RS Porsche on the twisting, turning 3.81 mile road course, which used the infield and part of the famed Daytona banks.

In 1962, Graham Shaw of Columbia, South Carolina, won the event in his Lister-Corvette, averaging 93.9 miles per hour. Charlie Kolb of Miami took the Whiteman trophy in both 1963 and 1964. Kolb pushed his tiny Lotus 23 to an average speed of 94.1 in 1963, and returned the following year in an RSK Porsche to average 94.9 for the victory.

Dan Gurney in the Lotus Ford follows Jo Schlesser in the Cobra Daytona coupe in 1965 Daytona Continental action.

Bill France, Jr., left, welcomes Indianapolis and Formula One great Dan Gurney to Daytona.

The Dan Gurney/Jerry Grant Lotus Ford being prepared for the 1965 Daytona Continental.

The Phil Hill/Joakim Bonnier Chaparral, 65, leads the Ken Miles/Lloyd Ruby Ford Mark II, 98, and the Walt Hansgen/Mark Donohue Ford in the 1966 24-hour early action. The Miles/Ruby car won that year.

A time exposure emphasises night-time action in the 1966 24-hour race.

Bob Grossman comes out of the tri-oval in the North American Racing Team Ferrari in the 1965 Daytona Continental.

Phil Hill did not finish in this Chaparral in 1967. Here car-builder Jim Hall tests the car prior to the 24-hour race.

A full field of Formula Fords move down the 18 degree home straight of the Daytona International Speedway.

Bill France beams approval over an attractive "unofficial" starter for a Daytona sports car race.

No time for sleep as pit crews work frantically to get their cars back into the 24-hour race.

Textile magnate John Fulp of Anderson, South Carolina, captured the big feature in 1965 in a Lola, and became the first man to average over 100 miles per hour, recording a whopping 103.8 mph. International driving star Peter Gregg topped the field in 1966, driving a Porsche Carrera six to an average speed of 100.5. In 1967, M.A. Kellner of Lecanto, Florida, averaged 97 mph to win the event in a sports racing Cobra 289.

Following Whiteman's death, Speedway officials announced that the event would continue as a memorial and tribute to the famous man. Ed Hugus won the first race after Whiteman's death, turning in a splendid performance with his Porsche-powered Tricor special to win at an average speed of 96.2 miles per hour.

Dave Heinz won the Whiteman race in 1969 in a McKee Chevrolet at a speed of 101.45; John Tremblay in a Camaro won in 1970 at 97.89 mph; Tom Fraser in a Lola was victorious the following year at 104.12, and Pete Harrison won the last event in 1972 in a Lola at a record speed of 110.27.

A pair of Porsches and a Ferrari sit beside the road course, awaiting some expensive repairs.

The 24 Hours of Daytona has only the LeMans race as its equal in length. But the first race—the three-hour version—was won by international favorite Dan Gurney in a Lotus 23. He crossed the finish line on power provided by his battery.

This beginning race provided a hint of what was to come, for the field included such famed drivers as Phil Hill, Jimmy Clark, Stirling Moss (who won the GT class with a fourth overall finish in a Ferrari Berlinetta), Oliver Gendebien, Roger Ward, Fireball Roberts and Jim Hall. Gurney averaged 103.664 mph, and covered 311.11 miles over the track-road circuit.

The 1963 race was also a three-hour one and this time Pedro Rodriguez, the diminutive Mexican star, drove a Ferrari to first place, covering 306.61 miles.

In 1964 the Daytona Continental, as it was still called, took the first of its strides toward bigger and better things. Speedway officials asked and were given permission to increase the length of the event to 2,000 kilometers (1243 miles). Phil Hill and Rodriguez co-drove a Ferrari to win, covering the distance at an average speed of 98.230 miles per hour. This race marked the first time the course had been employed for competition during darkness. It had been predicted by some skeptics that drivers would not be able to negotiate the high banks at night, but they were run at all-out speeds without serious mishap.

In 1965 Ford started its drive to end the stranglehold that Ferrari had on road racing. A Mark I Ford prototype, driven by Ken Miles and Lloyd Ruby, came in first with a record speed of 99.944 miles per hour.

The race went to 24 hours in 1966 when the FIA agreed to France's request that it be expanded into an event equal to LeMans. The best men and machines in the world assembled for this test of swiftness and stamina, of which 14 hours was run in the darkness. Ford proved its sweep in the 2,000 kilometers was no fluke by running 1-2-3, with Miles and Ruby again coming home the winners. This outstanding team covered 2,570.63 miles at an average speed of 108.02 mph.

In 1967 Ferrari, determined to put Ford in its place, made early tests of its new prototypes at Daytona, and then returned to take the top three places with Chris Amon and Lorenzo Bandini behind the wheel of the first place car. They covered 2,537.46 miles at an average speed of 105.688.

During these first years, the unobtrusive little German Porsches, usually with engines no larger than two litres, had been running well up among the leaders and had finished as high as fourth. But the Germans were soon to have their day.

Vic Elford of England and Jochen Neerspasch of Germany guided a streamlined new Porsche 907 prototype to victory in 1968. It was to open a period of nearly complete Porsche domination of the 24-hour event.

In 1969 Mark Donohue and Chuck Parsons survived a tremendous battle of attrition to take the Lola-Chevy to the winner's circle. Donohue and Parsons averaged 99.268 miles per hour in a grueling race that saw a seemingly unbeatable five-car Porsche team falter to mechanical ills during the long night hours.

Porsche was to lose but one more race in the history of the 24-hour event—the 1976 race when the Gregg/Redman/Fitzpatrick BMW won at an average speed of 104.04 miles per hour.

The Porsche victories were registered by Rodriguez and Kinnunen in 1970, Rodriguez and Jackie Oliver in 1971, Mario Andretti and Jackie Ickx in 1972, Peter Gregg and Hurley Haywood in 1973 and 1975 (there was no race in 1974 due to the energy crisis), Graves/Haywood/Helmick in 1977, Stommelen/Hezemans/Gregg in 1978 and Ongais/Field/Haywood in 1979.

In 1971 Bill France became irritated with the SCCA when they moved the Thanksgiving weekend event to Atlanta without consulting him. France had alternated with Riverside Raceway, giving drivers on each coast a better

International racing star David Hobbs has been a crowd-pleaser at Daytona.

and less-expensive crack at sports car racing. He felt the formula was working, so when he learned that the SCCA would be in Atlanta that year, he announced that he would still have the race at Daytona.

Hasty repairs are made to the Porsche of Pedro Rodriguez and Jackie Oliver during the 1971 24-hours.

Ronnie Bucknum in the Ferrari 512S during the 1971 24-hour race.

Eventual winner John Greenwood leads the pack through the tri-oval in the 1974 IMSA race.

Close order drill in the 1974 Camel 250 as the Ludwin Heimrath Porsche leads the Gang/Cook Porsche, 58, and the Ross/Evans Corvette.

Corvette patriarch Zora Arkus-Duntov, left, assists Victory Lane activities in the 1974 IMSA event as winner John Greenwood kibitzes.

John Bishop, president of International Motor Sports Association (IMSA). A number of IMSA-sanctioned events are held annually at the Daytona International Speedway.

He simply helped start a new sports car sanctioning body, the International Motor Sports Association (IMSA). Working with John Bishop, who became IMSA's president and guiding light, France lent moral and financial support. Today IMSA holds more than 40 professional races before nearly half a million spectators and has more than a dozen employees in its Bridgeport, Connecticut, offices.

IMSA's motto, "racing with a difference," has gained it worldwide recognition. One distinction is that its sole business is professional racing. All its efforts are directed at wheel-to-wheel feature competition with none of its energies expended on other activities. Another obvious IMSA difference is that in both its major racing series—one for Grand Touring and one for Racing Stock cars—the cars are easily recognized as based on familiar production cars. Anyone who knows a street Porsche when he meets one will

145

Dick Gail, center, of Champion Spark Plug Co., joins Peter Gregg and Hurley Haywood in Victory Lane in the 1975 24-Hour race.

The 1976 International Race of Champions. Benny Parsons was the eventual winner.

International hero Ronnie Peterson at Daytona in 1975.

Mario Andretti, right, and Al Unser uncork the champagne in Victory Lane following the 1978 Daytona International Race of Champions. Andretti won the race, Unser the championship.

1978 IMSA action at Daytona.

Bob Tullius relinquishes the wheel of the XJS Jaguar in the 1978 IMSA race.

The 1978 winning car in the 24-hour race, the Rolf Stommelmen and Tonie Hezemans entry, leads the Danny Ongais and Ted Field car. Ongais and Field teamed up with Hurley Haywood in the black Porsche to win the 1979 event.

Early infield action in the 1970 24-hour race.

Danni Ongais, left, photo-shy Ted Field, whose beard can be seen behind the trophy and Hurley Haywood, right are presented the trophy following their victory in the 1979 24-hour race. Holding the trophy, center, is John Sculley, Pepsico president.

recognize a turbocharged Porsche IMSA racer. A GT Corvette, Camaro or Monza is unmistakably defined by those popular Chevrolet lines. In the RS series, the cars are dead ringers for the imported and domestic compacts in the spectator parking lots.

The new Ford engine qualified for the 1967 Grand National season in the 119-inch wheelbase class, but with a weight minimum of 4427 pounds. Ford would be giving up 427 pounds over the pushrod-engined cars. Plans for using it were shelved. For one thing, the new rules allowed them to use two four-barrel carbs on their wedge engine and that should have been enough in their new, smaller aerodynamically cleaner Fairlane.

Qualifications for the 1967 five-hundred miler produced a combination of Smokey Yunick-Curtis Turner psyching that got to everyone. NASCAR rules stated that fenders could be cut away to provide clearance for the larger racing tires. Car-builders had always done just that. But when Smokey showed up with his black and gold Number 13 Chevelle, with all of the sheet metal intact, everybody, including the technical inspectors, raised their eyebrows. "You have to cut the fenders," someone said. "No, you don't *have* to cut them," Smokey said. "It just says you can if you *want* to."

They checked the rules and agreed that, by the letter of the law, he was right. So Curtis promptly took the car out and qualified it. With the extra sheet metal giving it a slightly better streamlining effect around the wheel openings (it trapped far less air) Curtis became the first man in history to qualify a car at three miles per minute. His average speed was 180.831.

And then they trimmed the sheet metal away.

Everybody in the pits went right into orbit. "Listen," they said, "You can't trim it now, and besides, you said you weren't going to do it at all."

"I didn't say I wasn't going to do it at all," said Smokey, "I just wasn't ready."

"Well, you can't do it after you qualify," they said.

"Check the rules," he replied. "It says you *can* cut the metal away. It doesn't say anywhere *when* you have to do it."

Smokey was right again, and Curtis' record qualifying speed stood. To make matters worse, Smokey went around the pits, telling everybody that he hadn't used his best engine. It terrorized the Ford people.

On race day, the psyching was all over and the moment of truth was at hand. Turner did lead the first lap, but Lee Roy Yarbrough, in a Dodge, went by him on the second lap; then Foyt, in a Ford, took over, then Baker in a Dodge. The top ten cars were running in a pack, passing and repassing everywhere on the track—the fans witnessing the fastest stock car race in history. Cars spun, gathered it up, and spun again.

The fast speeds began to take their toll. Cale damaged his suspension, avoiding a spin out in front of him on the 42nd lap. Foyt went out with clutch problems on the same lap; Turner, still in the running for first place at the 143rd lap, blew his engine, removing the top General Motors entry. The race settled down to a battle between Mario Andretti in a Ford, David Pearson in a Dodge and Darel Dieringer in a Ford, with Lorenzen running just behind them, waiting for someone to break or spin.

Dieringer was slowed by shock absorber problems and Pearson blew his engine at the 159th lap. Andretti and Lorenzen, both in Fairlanes, roared around the track, lap after lap, as if they were wired together. But they came up on Tiny Lund in a Plymouth, who was a lap behind but running fast. Andretti got past Lund, but Lorenzen took longer doing it, and the USAC star built up enough of a lead to take the checkered flag.

Cale dominated the 400 that year, but it was Richard Petty who stole the NASCAR spotlight for the season. It didn't seem to matter how quick anybody was on the other tracks all season, they simply could not catch Petty. By late summer he had won ten races in a row, which is a feat no one had ever even come close to. It began to look as if nobody else would ever win. When the season was over, Petty had run in 48 races and won an incredible 27 of them, finishing in the top ten 40 times.

When Chevrolet jumped into racing, Ford countered with a factory team managed by Peter DePaolo, left, former Indianapolis great. Here he chats with driver Ralph Moody, who later was half of the famous Holman and Moody racing enterprise.

A young Richard Petty, top photo, dreams of a racing career of his own following Daddy Lee's 1953 victory. By 1967, bottom photo, the dream had come true and a retired Lee Petty reflects on his own illustrious career.

Ray Fox was not only one of NASCAR's great car-builders, but he got right into the pit action as well.

Mario Andretti waves to the crowd from the 1967 five hundred winner's circle.

A sequence camera catches the violent crash of Johnny Roberts in the 1967 ARCA 250. Roberts was not seriously injured in the 35th lap crash.

153

Cale Yarborough switched to Wood Brothers and a Mercury in 1968 and the combination worked. He did not break Petty's mark of 27 victories, but he did manage to win $138,000 for the season, which was a record. His hard-charging driving ability, linked with the fabulous pit service, gave him a big advantage. In the 500, Cale came into the pits early in the race with ignition problems and, after diagnosing the situation, Leonard Wood dived into the driving compartment and replaced the part. Cale had lost three laps, but he roared out onto the track and, following an astounding feat of driving, caught the leaders, battling Lee Roy Yarbrough from the 89th lap to the end of the race. At the checkered flag, Cale was in front.

UP-UP AND AWAY FAST—That's the name of the game in NASCAR's tough Grand National Division. Pit crews can make up more time in the pits than a driver can on the track! Here gas flies out the overflow pipe of Buddy Baker's Charger as the Ray Fox crew changes two (2) tires and adds 21 gallons of gas in under 23 seconds.

1968 Daytona 500 winner Cale Yarborough: top left, leading the pack; bottom left, close up; and at right, the smiling victor.

The Firecracker for 1968 was again a Cale and Lee Roy show. Between them, they led all but nine laps, with Cale winning out after the half-way point. It was the third straight Daytona race victory for Cale, and he gave a lot of credit to his pit crew. In fact, from that point on, everybody in stock car racing used the Wood Brothers as the standard for pit excellence and speed. One observer noted, "The Pettys are like the Boy Scouts, they come 'prepared.' Their cars are right, but if anything happens during the race, that's usually it. But the Wood Brothers, that's different: If it happens during the race, they can get it going again."

Crowd-pleaser Bobby Johns was a 60s NASCAR star.

Nineteen-sixty-nine was confusing to racing fans for several reasons. For one, Lee Roy Yarbrough won both races at Daytona, causing people to look for the *spelling* of a name to see who won what. First it had been Yarborough for three races, and then Yarbrough for the next two.

Lee Roy won the 500 with an interesting strategy. He had been racing bumper-to-bumper with Charlie Glotzbach when he unexpectedly came into the pits with 20 laps to go. His pit crew mounted a softer compound Goodyear on the left rear wheel because the track surface had gotten super slick and he felt he needed more bite in the turns.

"That did it," said crew chief Herb Nab, "The tire was built to go about 30 laps, so we knew it would hold up for those last 20. We were ready to outrun anybody on the track."

He reduced Glotzbach's lead second by second and caught him on the third turn of the last lap. He went right on by him in the turn and beat him across the finish line in a thriller.

Winner Lee Roy Yarbrough at speed during 1969 Daytona 500.

The remains of Bobby Allison's car following the 1969 Firecracker 400.

Daytona, however, was not the big news in 1969. Bill France had built another superspeedway in the image of the mighty Daytona track.

"It was built mainly to help us with our cash flow problem in Daytona," France says. "It was impossible to have adequate cash coming in except for February and July race weeks. During the beginning of each fall we had to borrow $200,000 from the bank, so we opened Talladega to promote events during non-race periods in Daytona."

Speeds were increasing so rapidly at Daytona (both Cale and David Pearson had gone over 190 miles per hour in qualifying for the two 1969 races) that it was a concern to many. Talladega was even longer—2.66 miles—and had higher banks—33 degrees, so some predicted disaster. Most felt that tires and engines would blow sky high as the cars would surely surpass the 200 mile per hour mark.

The Professional Drivers Association, with Richard Petty as its president, had been formed with simple goals of improving pit conditions, garage area accommodations and assisting drivers with endorsements and personal appearances. But suddenly the PDA was the spokesman for the drivers who had lined up solidly against running at the new track.

They claimed that the speeds were so fast that the change in "g forces" caused them to black out momentarily in certain turns, a "pogo" effect, they called it. So the PDA announced that its members—which was the cream of the crop as far as NASCAR drivers went—would boycot the first Talladega race. France reacted more vehemently than he had ever done.

He held firm, demonstrating his legendary toughness, by running the race anyway, with a field of unknown drivers. The late Bobby Isaac was the only name driver to compete, and, to show his appreciation to Isaac, France presented him with a gold Rolex watch, suitably inscribed "Winners never quit, quitters never win."

Then France climbed into a borrowed Ford stock car, pulled on a crash helmet, buckled up and drove 176 miles per hour around the track.

"If a 60-year-old man can drive 176, surely our top drivers can do it safely at 20 miles over that," he proclaimed.

It was a hard point to refute.

France blamed the Ford Motor Company for the boycott.

"Plain, simple fact was that Ford was afraid that it was going to get beat by Dodge's new Daytona (and Plymouth's SuperBird) with the wings, so it (Ford) withdrew its cars," he said.

Ford did not comment.

France claimed that Bunkie Knudsen, president of Ford, had told him that factory Fords would run the first race at Talladega. But 48 hours before the Talladega 500, Henry Ford II fired Knudsen. Knudsen cancelled his plans to attend the race. So did the Ford factory cars.

The late Benny Kahn, who had been on the NASCAR scene from the beginning, told of yet another plan that was afoot, one to destroy France and perhaps even NASCAR. He wrote:

"In the late 60s, a Detroit real estate hustler with ambitions to take over stock car racing exploded on the scene: Larry LoPatin. In rapid fire order he built the two-mile track at Irish Hills (Michigan), another two-miler at College Station (Texas), and he acquired controlling interest in the tracks at Riverside and Atlanta.

"LoPatin immediately began a systematic campaign to downgrade France as Mr. Racing. He lacked racing background as well as patience. LoPatin sought an instant jackpot—or sooner! And in the plotting, LoPatin encouraged top name race drivers in NASCAR to organize and sever their close ties with Bill France and his organization.

"LoPatin had hidden but powerful support from aloof Jacque Passino, who headed the rich Ford Motor Co. factory race operations. Passino wanted to dictate new rules to Bill France, instead of vice versa. Ford was spending millions on racing under Passino's guidance but Chrysler was spending less and getting more results under the astute direction of the late Ronnie Householder.

" 'The Professional Drivers Assn. was born, with the quiet approval of Passino. LoPatin was instrumental in it,' reflects France.

PDA flexed its muscle in August, 1969, when France scheduled his inaugural 500-mile race on the then brand new 2.66-mile Talladega track. The name stars of PDA boycotted the race. They called the track unsafe. Passino pulled out FoMoCo factory cars."

The race turned out to be a safe, crowd-pleasing thriller, with scarcely-known Richard Brickhouse the winner. The PDA lost the round, LoPatin's race track empire crumbled. Bankruptcy swallowed it.

The race drivers and France shook hands, and picked up the thread of their mutually beneficial relationship where it had been dropped. Larry LoPatin? He quit racing.

France had again displayed his power. Shortly after, someone asked him if he considered himself a "czar."

"I don't know what a czar is," he replied. "If being a czar is owing a lot of money, then I'm a czar. But I'm proud of NASCAR and what it's done. It was founded because there was a need for it. There were unpaid hospital bills, drivers not getting paid, cars being raced that you might say provided inadequate protection for contestants. NASCAR has brought rules and regulation and sense to racing. I don't think it's perfect, but up to now, it's the best organization to come along in motor sports."

France formed the International Speedway Corporation, which included both the Daytona and Talladega tracks. When asked by the *Orlando Sentinel* how many shares of stock the France family held in ISC and how many were held by Union Oil, France answered: "The France family holding in the International Speedway Corporation, which includes Talladega, is 1,250,000 one dollar shares. Union Oil holds one million."

Meanwhile, David Pearson was winning his third national championship and the very last NASCAR dirt track was being run. Richard Petty won. It brought back fond memories to many NASCAR drivers who had raced on the old dirt tracks. Perhaps it was comic relief to high speed problems.

"Good dirt track drivers aren't necessarily good asphalt drivers," says Buddy Baker. "I know a lot of people who quit racing when the dirt tracks in their area closed down."

Alf Knight, the Atlanta International Raceway superintendent, said, "The dirt tracks may close, but the legends will linger on.

"I remember a time over in Chattanooga when Olin Allen was driving for Harvey Jones. Old Olin and a driver named Happy Homes got to mixing it up on the track and Happy knocked Olin off the track.

"Harvey picked up a brick and went over on the back stretch. When Happy came by, he threw it right through his windsheild. When he came to the pits it was like a world war had broke out. Everybody got to fighting. They just let them fight until everybody was so tired they couldn't fight no more.

"I reckon one of the best things that ever happened to racing was NASCAR. NASCAR don't let them fight no more."

Pete Hamilton winning the 500-miler in 1970 in a Petty Plymouth SuperBird.

Meanwhile back on the Daytona asphalt, speed kept going up. Cale Yarborough qualified for the 1970 Daytona 500 at 194.015 miles per hour in his Mercury. The winged Mopars were almost as fast. And, as one could predict, race day produced almost as many yellow flags as there were cars. The speeds took their toll with engines.

When the smoke cleared, a 28-year-old New Englander, Pete Hamilton, was out in front in the *other* Petty Plymouth Superbird. David Pearson, the old pro, tried valiantly to catch Hamilton in the closing stages, but the weird-looking winged car was just too much. Hamilton picked up $46,500 for his victory.

By July 4, Ford had their special racing-designed Talladega model running as well as the Plymouths and Dodges. The long-nose Talladega of David Pearson had built up a commanding lead late in the race, with teammate Donnie Allison, in an identical car, running second. When Pearson blew a tire and brushed the wall, it left Allison in front of a trio of Dodges driven by Buddy Baker, brother Bobby Allison and Charlie Glotzbach, but none of them could catch the Ford. Donnie had led only seven laps of the race by the time he got the checkered flag.

The torrid speeds at Daytona and Talladega prompted NASCAR and Bill France to take a long look at the situation. What they saw frightened them. What they did made better races for the fans, drivers, car-owners, manufacturers and, well, just about everybody including the insurance companies. He slowed them down.

NASCAR came up with a simple but ingenious device called the "restrictor plate." It was a small plate that fit between the carburetor and the intake manifold, reducing the flow of fuel and cutting the power of the engines. The plates—with different size openings for different engines—were not only to bring speed down, but to make racing more competitive, giving all the cars an equal chance. France said:

"Its not a matter of the track being faster than the car or vice versa," he explained. "Frankly, we found ourselves in the awkward position of having races continually interrupted by blown engines and tires. Speeds were increased more by body design than horsepower.

"In order to cut down on blown engines and tire wear, all of which were extremely expensive for our independent drivers, we decided to slow down.

Buddy Baker, left, and David Pearson inspect the controversial restrictor plates that puzzled mechanics in early 70s NASCAR events.

"And it has worked. The restrictor plates took the edge off the pressure. Drivers are now getting longer engine life and much better tire wear. You might say the restrictor plates were both a safety and economic move."

As usual, the manufacturers didn't agree with France.

Chrysler said: "France looks at racing differently than we do. We want to get an extra advantage that will let us win. So does Ford. But Bill wants everything to be even, which gives us two guarantees. One, we know he'll never let our cars get too slow. But, two, we also know he'll never let them get too fast. Essentially we view stock car racing as a sport. He views it as entertainment."

Mopar drivers claimed that the plates gave Ford an unfair advantage. Ford said it was designed to bring Chevrolet back into racing. There was more action off the track than there was on. But it did slow things down. And the factories got out of racing.

Cale Yarborough of Timmonsville, S.C., leads the fastest field of stock car drivers in the country into the high-banked west turn of Daytona International Speedway during the 1970 Daytona 500. Yarborough had qualified his Wood Brothers prepared Mercury Cyclone at better than 194 miles per hour for the pole position.

Buddy Baker, always a charger, takes the direct approach to cooling off, too. He just grabbed the hose from the pitcrew and staged his own cool-down.

Nineteen-seventy-one was the year that Richard Petty won more than $300,000 and became the first million dollar winner in the sport of stock car racing. And he got started that year in the Daytona 500, although there wasn't one of the 100,000 fans that was sure about the outcome until the checkered flag dropped.

There were 48 lead changes among 11 different drivers during the race, with only one driver (Petty) leading more than 15 laps at one clip. At the end, Buddy Baker in a Dodge and A.J. Foyt in a Mercury were breathing right down the tailpipe of the Petty Plymouth.

The Firecracker 400 that year was even more crowd-pleasing. The hard luck king, Bobby Isaac, finally won a clear-cut superspeedway race. Isaac, who had risen from poverty to drive a race car, had a checkered career in Grand National. After several years of trying to land a top ride, he finally connected with a Ray Nichels factory Dodge in 1964, only to have the company pull out of racing. The following year, he landed a ride in a factory Ford, just in time to see them pull out.

The next year he got the driver's assignment in the independent Junior Johnson car, but several fence-busting episodes bounced him out of that. Perhaps he was too enthusiastic about winning.

Isaac had won another superspeedway race, this one at Texas, but it had been somewhat jaded because Buddy Baker had had a commanding lead when he crashed late in the race, leaving Victory Lane to Isaac. Bobby had always felt short-changed in that one. But the 1971 Firecracker was no fluke. It did, however, look for a while as if the Isaac bad luck had returned. He had to start 21st in the 40 car field because his racer—the K & K Insurance Dodge—had arrived late. And he ran out of gas early in the race, costing him valuable time. Isaac made up the lost time and built up a decisive lead over Richard Petty late in the race. Then a hood pin broke loose and the

Ted Webbe was one of the earliest "racing voices." He followed NASCAR racing for many years.

A tired Bobby Isaac poses with the winner's trophy and a trio of beauty queens following the 1971 Firecracker 400.

right rear side of the hood began to flap. Two laps later, the buffeting wind of the 180 miles per hour pace snapped a second pin. When a third one let go the next lap, Isaac cut his speed 20 miles an hour and crossed his fingers. If the hood came off it meant the windshield, possibly a crash and certainly the race.

Petty whacked large chunks from his once comfortable lead, and on the last lap almost caught him, but the lone remaining hood pin held and Isaac was flagged the winner.

"I just kept hoping that every lap would be the last one," said Isaac. "Even when I got the white flag signaling the start of the final lap, I still wasn't sure Petty couldn't catch me. I was running as hard as I could under

Walter Ballard flips in the tri-oval during the 500 in 1972.

the conditions, but that loose hood cost me 15 or 20 miles an hour. The wind was getting under the hood and picking the front end off the ground."

The 1972 five hundred-miler was, for all practical purposes, over after the 81st lap. Up until that time it had been a frantic battle between A.J. Foyt

Buddy Baker heads for the pits after blowing his engine in the 1972 Firecracker 400.

in the Wood Brothers Mercury and the Petty team cars, driven by Buddy Baker and Richard.

Isaac, starting from the pole, had left the race early with ignition problems, giving Foyt the lead. By the 18th lap, Petty had moved to second place and Baker, who had also worked his way up through the pack, was running third. In perhaps the only exciting moment of the day, Walter Ballard clipped the front end of the Baker Dodge coming out of the fourth turn. The collision flipped Ballard on the roof of his Ford and slammed Baker into the wall. Ballard's car slid on its top for 500 yards and then flipped three times with parts flying everywhere. Meanwhile, Buddy Arrington slammed into the side of Baker's car. The yellow flag caused a minor Petty-Foyt bash, as Richard slid into Foyt's back bumper, but neither car was badly damaged.

By lap 28, there was nobody in contention but Foyt and Petty. They had swapped the lead nine times and the fans yelled for more. But it was all over quickly when Petty pulled behind the pit wall with a broken valve spring. Foyt established a record speed of 161.550 miles per hour, with Charlie Glotzbach a full lap behind him in the Cotton Owens Dodge.

Nineteen-seventy-two's Firecracker 400 was the beginning of a late race show that would be repeated many times over the years—the Richard Petty-David Pearson minuet that has always kept the fans on their feet.

The final caution flag of the race ended at lap 141, and from that point Petty and Pearson—with an occasional excursion from Bobby Allison—exchanged the lead 50 times in the last 48 laps. The fans had long forgotten that there were seats at the Daytona International Speedway. For one thing, the three car battle was what Bill France had dreamed of. It pitted the big three, Petty's Mopar, Pearson's FoMoCo and Allison's Chevrolet.

"The finish reminded me of Kansas City and that sudden death American Football League championship game," said grand marshall Don Shula, coach of the Miami Dolphins.

"It reminded me that I am too old for this sort of thing," said crew chief Leonard Wood.

Every lap in the late stages of the race was more emotional than the one

before. On the last lap, everyone, including Pearson, expected Petty to snap out of his draft and sling-shot ahead of the Mercury, but he didn't. As Pearson crossed the finish line, Petty's radiator was alongside Pearson's door. Allison was a car length and a half behind them.

Pearson said Petty "goofed," in not sling-shotting. Petty said he was merely battling for second place and that his car was not fast enough to pass Pearson. Some wondered if an earlier attempt by Petty to pass Pearson, which resulted in Petty being forced to brush the concrete wall had any bearing on the last lap strategy. It certainly wasn't the last time the pair would hammer at each other on the final lap.

It was appropriate that Bill France would step down as president of NASCAR in 1972, because it gave Bill, Jr., a chance to start the *second* 25 years at the helm of the world's largest racing organization. And Bill, Jr., had a

Darrell Waltrip is the youngest member of the NASCAR *superstar ranks.*

Wendell Scott became the first black NASCAR *star, driving the entire circuit for many years.*

Bobby Allison reflects on another reason for winning races.

The Allison brothers in and out of action. Donnie, 88, after slamming into the wall during the 1973 Talladega 500 and Bobby, 12, spinning toward the infield as Randy Tissot, 74, sneaks underneath.

good hold on the reins in typical France fashion as NASCAR celebrated its Silver Anniversary in 1973. Ably helping him as vice president was his brother, Jim.

Further rules changes the previous year were still an irritant to many, and Bill, Jr., fielded these complaints with much the same toughness that his father had in years before. Smaller carburetors had been ruled in to bring the large engines down to a more competitive standpoint with the small block racers. Many felt it was a ruling to bring Chevrolet race cars back to the front of NASCAR after a long absence.

"It figures," said one long-time observer, "that the Frances want Chevy back. I mean, look at all the Chevy fans it will bring to the races."

More than 103,000 fans were on hand for the 1973 Daytona 500 (perhaps the Chevy speculation had been right) and they witnessed a fierce battle between two teammates, Richard Petty and Buddy Baker—the STP racing team.

The pair had been racing, bumper to bumper, for the last 50 laps of the race. They had out distanced the entire remainder of the field by more than two laps. Petty, the old pro, outsmarted Baker, when he couldn't pull away from him. Roaring out of the fourth turn, Petty dove his Dodge into the pits, slamming on his brakes so hard that the car threw a cloud of tire smoke. Petty's crew dumped in five gallons of gas—enough to get him to the checkered flag, if he could get back in front—and he was out in 8.4 seconds. He had less than a quarter of a mile to make up on Baker. On the next lap, Baker took the more conventional method of pitting, by slowing down in the third turn and coasting into the pits. "After all," one of Petty's pit crew said, "he's got 271 less races under his belt then Richard."

The 10 second stop by Baker, plus the much longer slow down to enter the pits, put Baker one quarter of a mile *behind* Richard. In trying to catch up, Baker blew his engine. Petty won by two laps over Bobby Isaac.

"I taught Buddy all the tricks that I knew about drafting and setting up guys to pass them," said Petty. "But I didn't tell him that beating a guy in the pits is just as good as beating him out on the track.

"If I had, Buddy might be here collecting all this money instead of me."

The 1973 Firecracker version of the Petty-Pearson road show was somewhat less dramatic than the others had been—or the ones to follow. Pearson, who had been leading Petty most of the race, simply pulled away in the last laps to beat the Dodge by 300 yards, and it brought a terse comment from Petty after the race.

"I don't ever like to lose," he said, "but I hate like hell to get played with. Pearson just played with me up until about 10 laps to go and then he just drove off and left me. I guess he just decided to quit messing around and go on."

"Shoot," said Pearson, "I was driving just as hard all day as it would go. Everything just fell into place for us in the last 15 laps. I think Richard must have got caught in traffic or something."

Baker was third; the year's Indianapolis 500 winner, Gordon Johncock, was fourth and Benny Parsons was fifth.

There was more controversy about the rules changes than about Pearson's supposed sandbagging, however. Many had felt that the changes were brought about not only to help the Chevys but to clip the high-flying Pearson's wings. It obviously didn't work on either count.

"I don't know who had the fastest cars on the track," Pearson said, "but I think if you'll check the times of all the cars for the day, the Chevys were probably the cars with the quickest speeds. The rules change definitely hurt us.

"Y'all saw the destruction of the Hemi here today," said Baker. "I had no power down the chute at all. My car today ran like the old sled I ran to second-place here in 1965. What NASCAR did with the rules change was make a second-rate machine out of a great race car."

What did his opposition say? Well, they sort of agreed.

"I still feel they cut the Hemis too much," said Glen Wood, "but I also must admit I've got a pretty smart mechanic. If anybody can cope with a rules change like this, it's Leonard (Wood). Fortunately for us, all of them don't have that good a mechanic."

The major problem that threatened the Daytona 500 in 1974—and all of motorsports, for that matter—had nothing to do with racing. The nation faced a gasoline shortage and the resulting crisis placed fear in race track promoters all over the country. There was even some talk of stopping auto racing. But Bill France, Jr., armed himself with one good statistic and prepared to go to the nation's capital if necessary. The statistic? "It takes less fuel to run a 500-mile auto race than it does to fly the Washington Redskins to a pro football game on the West Coast. And that's *all* the cars involved."

It was an impressive figure, but more than that, it indicated that NASCAR was not going to roll over and play dead.

France made one concession to the crisis. He cut the Daytona 500 to 450 miles for that year.

The parking lot on race day looked as if the crowd was less than half of what France had hoped for, but inside, it was the same old packed-house. Because of the fuel crisis people had doubled up in cars to conserve gasoline. More than 100,000 showed up. And they got a good show. Early in the race Hershell McGriff, driving a Petty-built Dodge, sponsored by a state tourist commission, flipped in the backstretch, turning the Wild, Wonderful West Virginia car into what looked like 50 miles of bad road.

Several other crashes narrowed the field, but something crowd-pleasing was happening on the track. The *Chevrolet* of Bobby Allison was running with Richard Petty. Allison passed Petty when the Dodge cut a tire and had to pit, and it appeared the Chevy would win the race. It streaked along, almost effortlessly, until an exploded engine on Bob Burcham's car littered the track with pieces of metal. Allison hit one, exploding a tire and sending the Chevy into a fierce slide. He gathered it up without hitting the wall, but the time he lost limping back around to his pits gave Petty plenty of time to roar into first place and win the race. Keep in mind, nobody has ever won the race twice. It was Petty's *fifth* victory.

Cale Yarborough is surrounded by the Union 76 Race Stoppers in victory lane after he won the second 112.5 mile qualifying race for the 1974 Daytona 500.

These sequence shots show step-by-step how the Wood brothers helped David Pearson win the 1974 Firecracker 400.

Spectators had come to expect a last lap Petty-Pearson battle, and the 1974 Firecracker gave them the biggest thrill yet. It also caused Petty to accuse Pearson of pulling a "dangerous and unnecessary" maneuver.

Petty, whose Dodge appeared slightly slower than the Mercury, was drafting Pearson as the cars came out of the fourth turn to take the white flag. As they roared down the front chute Pearson backed off the throttle completely, forcing Petty to swerve his Dodge into the lead.

The move had been calculated by Pearson to get Petty out of his draft at that point and to prevent him from sling-shotting to victory on the last turn of the last lap. Petty had two choices, swing *around* Pearson or *into* him.

Pearson spotted Petty a 300-yard lead, but he gunned the Mercury into Petty's air foil coming down the back stretch and set up the sling-shot. The two cars exited turn four and headed for the finish line. Pearson swung low to pass, and Petty crowded him down near the grass, trying to keep him back. But Pearson stayed on it and crossed the finish line a hair in front.

Meanwhile, behind them, fighting for third place, was an even closer battle. Buddy Baker's Ford and Cale Yarborough's Chevrolet crossed the finish line wheel-to-wheel. The photo finish camera, operating at 500 frames per second, verified what everybody thought, an absolute dead heat.

The R.J. Reynolds Tobacco Company entry into Grand National racing played a major role in preventing the sagging economy from seriously affecting NASCAR events. By 1975, the Winston Cup series was firmly established and it proved to be the greatest asset to Daytona of anything in history. Everybody at R.J. Reynolds, from Board Chairman William D. Hobbs down, lined up solidly behind NASCAR and helped pull them through the 1974-75 fuel and economy crisis.

If Winston had helped get the race going, Pearson provided what the fans had come to see, another 500 thriller.

Petty had been clearly the fastest car on the track, but an over-heating radiator had dropped him back. With a few laps to go, he had the problem solved and was again the fastest car on the track—in sixth place at the time, however. Benny Parsons, the humble ex-taxi driver, realized Petty's speed and jumped into his draft. The maneuver brought the second-place Parsons to within two seconds, with two laps remaining.

Pearson roared out of turn two and down the backstretch, where he ran up behind the Chevrolets of Richie Panch and Cale Yarborough. They momentarily appeared to ignore the blue and yellow "move over" flag, and Pearson darted left to pass. Then back to the right. But Pearson's right rear

The 1974 Firecracker 400 dead-heat finish for third place between Cale Yarborough, 11, and Buddy Baker.

From left, Richard Petty, car-builder Bud Moore, Buddy Baker and Bobby Allison in a typical pre-race bull session.

Donnie Allison and Miss Speedweeks '75 open activities at the Speedway.

1975 Daytona 500 fourth lap crash removed nine cars from the race, including Warren Tope, 81, Bruce Hill, 47, Dan Daugherty, 35, Dick Trickle, 75, and Grant Adcox, 41.

Lennie Pond takes on left side rubber during the 500 in 1975.

Marty Robbins was proclaimed "wall tester" after this 1975 crash. He had hit the wall in the same spot in 1973.

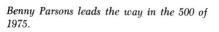

Benny Parsons leads the way in the 500 of 1975.

Daytona P.R. Chief Jim Foster conducts one of many tours around the Speedway.

176

Richard Petty makes his final pit stop before winning the 1975 Firecracker 400.

fender made contact with Yarborough's left front fender as Pearson went by, sending the Mercury into a 180 mile an hour slide down the backstretch.

After the race, an infuriated Pearson snapped, "I got spun out, but I'd just as soon not talk about it. People who were watching know who did it. They know who was over there with me."

Yarborough said, "I don't know whether he cut back too soon or what, but he clipped me and spun out. I hate it happened to him."

In the 1975 Firecracker 400 Richard Petty reached down into his bag of tricks again. Petty had qualified badly and it took him most of the afternoon to catch Buddy Baker. But 13 laps from the finish, Petty was right on Baker's bumper. An earlier pit stop by the two cars had left Petty's slightly faster. It had been Manuever Number One in his trick file. Baker pitted for the final time on lap 138 and took on right side tires. Petty pitted two laps later and had left side rubber changed.

"I was running so high on the track that I figured the right side tires wouldn't be in the greasy part of the track, while the left side would," said Petty after the race.

Baker said, "If we had it to do all over again, you better believe we would have changed left side tires (which normally don't get nearly as much wear as right side rubber). You just don't beat a guy like Petty if everything isn't working just right."

But it was the final manuever—the one with 13 laps to go—that gave Petty his first Firecracker win.

Baker zoomed by Petty going into the third turn and, in the process, went four or five car lengths deeper into the turn than he should have to exit properly.

"I knew that Buddy had to back completely off the accelerator to correct himself in that corner," said Petty. "So, soon as his car cleared mine, I ducked low and poured on the coal. My car was handling better than his in the turns. That shot me back in the lead."

Baker never caught him again. The victory sent Petty well on his way to his sixth NASCAR driving championship—and his second million dollars.

Bill France received the ultimate stock car racer's honor in 1976. He was elected to the National Motorsports Press Association's Hall of Fame, joining many of his old pals, like Curtis Turner, Joe Weatherly, Fireball Roberts, Red Byron and Lee Petty. There is no question in anybody's mind that France would have been there years before—perhaps first—but the requirements for eligibility, aside from the vote of the members, required the inductee to have been retired for at least four years.

Paul A. Cameron (left) and David Pearson in victory lane following Pearson's victory in the 1976 Daytona 500. Cameron is President of Purolator, Inc., the sponsor of Pearson's car.

A traffic jam at 150 miles per hour during the early stages of the 1976 International Race of Champions at Daytona.

Cecil Gordon after his crash with Janet Guthrie in the 1976 Firecracker 400.

Janet Guthrie drove in 19 NASCAR races in 1977 in her Kelly Girl Chevrolet.

Pearson had had the incredible foresight to push in his clutch when the car hit the wall, and he threw the car into neutral. His engine was still running, so he dumped it into first and stood on it. Grass and dirt erupted from behind his rear wheels, and the car sloshed back and forth, heading for the track. Petty's Dodge was dead. He had slid backwards, stopping 100 yard short of the finish line. Had he spun past the line, even off in the grass, he would have been the winner. But he hadn't and Pearson gunned the Mercury toward the starter, who held the checkered flag over his head. There was a look of total disbelief on his face as the Wood brothers car limped past him.

It looked as if Pearson should be rolling into a junkyard instead of Victory Lane, but the jubilant Silver Fox pulled himself from the car, flashing a wry smile at his sponsors, the Purolator people.

Later Petty went to Pearson and said, "I'm really sorry I hit you, David." Pearson stoically replied, "Aw, that's okay, Richard, you didn't do it on purpose."

It is the stuff of which legends are made.

The Cale Yarborough-Junior Johnson combination was too much for competitors in the 1976 Firecracker. The Johnson-prepared Chevy easily ran away from everybody, giving Cale his third July 4 victory. Cale survived an eight-car pileup on the 34th lap that happened when Baker blew an engine right in front of him.

"I was right on Buddy's bumper when his engine blew. I couldn't even see Buddy's car for the oil that covered my windshield, but I didn't slide, so I got through."

Eight other cars didn't survive, including, ironically, Buddy's father, Buck.

The beginning and the end. The Ormond Garage, where the first beach racers worked on their machines, had been the object of a campaign to perserve the "original Gasoline Alley," when fire broke out in December 1976. Within minutes the historic structure was reduced to rubble.

Benny Parsons gets 20-second service.

1977 Champion Cale Yarborough.

Chief Scorer and Timer Joe Epton, right, has
been with NASCAR since the beginning.

Miss Firebird, Winky Louise, a major reason many drivers rushed to the winner's circle.

Two members of the Alabama Gang, Bobby Allison, left, and brother Donnie discuss pre-race strategy. The third member of the Gang is fellow Hueytown resident Neil Bonnett.

Ray Hendrick, 01, finished fifth in the 1977 Sportsman race after hitting the wall. Jack Ingram, 45, and Billy McGinnis, 84, avoided contact.

Two of the Union Oil Race stoppers chat at the ARCA racer of Joe Millikan.

These seven drivers all have different driving styles and as you can see, different driving shoes. Can you match the drivers with their shoes? The drivers, left to right; Buddy Baker, Benny Parson, Neil Bonnett, Lenny Pond, David Pearson, Cale Yarborough and Bobby Allison.

ANSWER: Pond, Bonnett, Baker, Allison, Parsons, Yarborough, Pearson.

Modified pit stop action in 1977.

Richard Petty, 43, leads Bobby Allison through the corner in the 1977 Firecracker 400, which Petty won.

Kyle Petty, right, shares the 1977 Firecracker Victory Lane with his father, Richard, and the Hurst beauty queens.

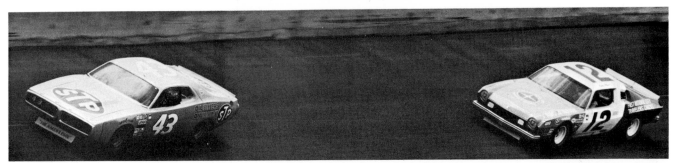

Chevrolet demonstrated its supremacy in the 1977 Daytona 500 as Yarborough breezed around the track for a victory. It wasn't the only breeze of the day, however.

"The wind was so strong," says Yarborough, "that it just picked the car up in the second and third turns. I was just plain flying."

Words about the Chevys flew faster than Cale *or* the wind.

"I couldn't have caught him (Yarborough)," said Pearson. "He had too much horsepower. You know something's wrong when you can't draft by a car."

"I couldn't stay on 'em (the Chevrolets)," said Petty. "I couldn't run good enough really to draft 'em."

More than one driver complained about the rules changes. They contended it gave the Chevys—particularly the aerodynamically slick Lagunas—a big edge. The controversy continued as the Chevys proceeded to clean up all the hardware in the NASCAR circuit.

Petty got his Dodge act together in July, long enough to win the 1977 firecracker going away, in a race that was halted at one point for two hours by the Florida monsoon. But a drought was to follow. It was to be Petty's last victory for a season and a half. Most blamed his new Dodge Magnum.

"It must not be as slick as it looks," said one observer, " 'cause ol' Richard ain't been to the well in a long time."

Richard Petty, 43, Darrell Waltrip, 88, and David Pearson, 21, crash in Turn Four during the 1978 Daytona 500. The crash eliminated Petty and Pearson from the race.

Buddy Baker accepts a $1,000 check from Busch beer for grabbing the Daytona pole and setting a new track record of 196.049 miles-an-hour as Neil Bonnett looks on. It was a Busch day for Baker at Daytona as he also won the $50,000 top prize in the $150,000 Busch Clash of '79, the 50-mile dash for the nine drivers who won pole positions in 1978.

First lap action following the green flag.

Kenny Roberts in Victory Lane in Daytona following the 200 of 1978.

W. M. (Monty) Roberts III, marketing manager for Busch beer, left, and Lin Kuchler, executive vice president of NASCAR, review the Busch Beer Trophy for the 1979 season. The trophy is awarded to the driver who most often wins the pole position in qualifying for the 30 Winston Grand National races on the NASCAR circuit.

Petty agreed, because during the 1978 season, he switched cars—to a Chevrolet.

NASCAR stepped in with yet another rule change—to even things up again. This time they all but eliminated the Lagunas by forcing them to run with restrictor plates. The Chevy drivers switched to the less aerodynamically-clean Monte Carlo. And the Chevy fans and drivers screamed. Somewhere along the line, there must have been a lot of people saying, "Hey, this is where I came in."

Bobby Allison, driving a Ford Thunderbird that he called a "luxury liner," won the 1978 Daytona 500. It was the first time since 1959 that a Thunderbird had won a Grand National race, so perhaps it *was* where a lot of people came in.

Petty wasn't close enough at the finish for the semi-annual melee with Pearson, but Cale Yarborough, driving an Oldsmobile with a Chevy engine—a combination that Junior Johnson cleverly found to resemble the Laguna characteristics—filled in for Petty. He set Pearson up for the slingshot in turn four, but, by the time they got to the corner, Baxter Price's Chevrolet was in the way, and Cale could not make his move. He finished right on Pearson's bumper. Petty's fourth place finish was good enough to push him over the three million dollar mark in winnings, however.

Undoubtly the biggest news as 1979 Speed Weeks opened was a Petty. Not Lee. Not Richard. But Richard's 18-year-old son, Kyle. One year earlier, Kyle had stunned everybody, including his daddy, when he announced on network television that he was going to be a race driver. So Richard had put him in the year-old Dodge Magnum that he had qualified for the 1978 Daytona 500 at 183 miles per hour. The Pettys were at Daytona to test their new car, so Kyle took the Dodge around the tri-oval. At 184.5 miles per hour.

Richard then took the car out to see how in the world the kid had done it, and went 190 in the process, prompting Kyle to say, "Well, it looks like I'm gonna' have to do a little better if I'm gonna' run with Daddy." And he went 187. "Whoa," Richard said.

Daytona Mayor Lawrence Kelly watches as Bill France installs the sign in front of the Speedway, proclaiming the street "Bill France Boulevard," in honor of the city's most illustrious resident.

Kyle entered the ARCA 200 in 1979 in the Magnum and, what else, he won—the first race he ever entered. So, as NASCAR went into its 31st year of competition, a third generation Petty was on hand—and two second generation Frances were at the helm.

A second generation Baker, Buddy, broke the qualifying record for the track as he sailed around the tri-oval at 196.049 in an Oldsmobile. He gave much of the credit for his speed to the fact that the track had been resurfaced for the first time in its 21-year history.

A passel of Pettys celebrate third-generation driver Kyle's victory in the 1979 ARCA race. Kyle, center, his father, Richard, right, and grandfather, Lee, left, show their joy as Kyle wins the first race he ever enters. Three generations of Petty wives join them in Victory Lane.

Bobby Davis, 91, and Bobby Fisher, 71, collide during the 1979 ARCA race. Also involved in the mishap was defending champ Marvin Smith, 1.

Trouble in the pits for Buddy Baker in the 500 of 1979 as both ends of the Olds are opened up.

Ed Kretz rides the restored first winner around the Daytona track in 1979 pre-race activities. This is the same Indian bike on which he won the initial event in 1937 on the beach.

The Interscope Porsche in the early morning hours of the 24-hour Pepsi Challenge.

A night pit stop during the 1979 24-hour race.

The spectacular and fiery crash of Joe Frasson in the 1979 Sportsman race horrified spectators, but Frasson walked away from it. The Marion Cox Mercury had been around since 1968 and was called the "Never on Sunday" car because car owners refused to race it on the Sabbath.

Daytona has built a reputation for exciting finishes—thanks to Petty and Pearson—but the 1979 finish in the 500 made fans forget about all the others. A six-car pileup on the 55th lap had taken Pearson from the race, and by the final lap the closest Petty could get was third.

Apparently the two lead cars at the time, Donnie Allison and Cale Yarborough, both in Olds', felt it was up to them to uphold the heart-stopping last lap action that had become a Daytona trademark.

Cale had been drafting Donnie for a few laps. As they thundered down the backstretch, the crowd could sense what was coming, and they rose in unison, unaware of how *much* excitement was in store for them.

Cale pulled the Citicorp Olds out of the draft and the slingshot propelled him forward. He was between Donnie and the apron, down low. They roared down the chute, side by side, at nearly 200 miles an hour. Allison made *his* move. In an apparent attempt to bluff, he pulled left toward Yarborough. Yarborough did not back off. Allison moved a little closer. There was the sound of grinding metal as the two cars snapped at each other. Yarborough was in the dirt, but he still had his foot in it. NASCAR drivers are not easily intimidated.

The car hit again and bounced off, and Cale went farther into the dirt, and then he yanked his steering wheel hard right and the cars hit a third time. Fused together, they slid wildly toward the outer concrete wall. Cale jerked the wheel hard left, in an attempt to break loose before the crash, but it didn't work. Both cars smashed into the wall and rebounded across the track and into the infield.

Starter Chip Warren gets a bird's eye view of the Lennie Pond crash in a 1979 qualifying race.

The draft, which was discovered at Daytona.

Cale Yarborough, 11, about to pull alongside Donnie Allison in the last lap of the 1979 Daytona 500. Seconds later the two collided.

Richard Petty, 43, and Darrell Waltrip, 88, on their way to the checkered flag in the 1979 Daytona 500. Petty won with an average speed of 143.977 mph.

The 52nd Lap crash that took David Pearson and Bruce Hill out.

The thrill of victory—driver Buddy Baker and his wife and crew celebrate after winning the $150,000 Busch Clash of '79, the richest race per mile in stock car racing history. Herb Nab, team manager of the Spectra Olds that Baker drives, holds up the winner's trophy flanked by Baker and Monty Roerts—the Busch beer marketing manager who came up with the idea for the 50-mile dash for the nine drivers who won Busch Pole Awards during the 1978 Winston Cup season.

The IROC field comes out of the fourth turn at Daytona with two NASCAR stars, Parsons and Allison, in front.

Could it be Petty and Pearson again? No, this time, the gladiators were not as sanguine. In fact, Cale exploded from the car, looking for someone to break in two. Bobby Allison, who had stopped at the crash scene after Richard Petty had been flagged the winner of his sixth 500 (still nobody else had ever won even *two*), climbed from his car to see if his brother was all right. Cale punched him. And then Donnie.

"It's the worst thing I've ever seen in racing," says Cale. "Bobby waited so he could block me (Bobby was two laps behind the leaders). They double-teamed me. It was the worst thing I ever saw. My left wheels were over in the dirt and Donnie knocked me even farther. He carried me into the grass. I started spinning and Donnie started spinning. Donnie denied it when I asked him why he did it. He bowed up, so I took a swing at him."

Petty compared it with the crash he had with Pearson in 1976.

"Hey, we were more professional than those two. We at least got through turns three and four before we wrecked. And we did it over here in front of the grandstands, where everybody could see."

"Ah, I don't know. Curtis had as active a brain and as quick a reaction as anybody, but I wouldn't say that he was any better than, say, Richard Petty, day in and day out—or any of our top drivers today." The voice is that of Bill France as he sits in the spacious family room of the home on the banks of the Halifax, 32 years after he had started NASCAR. He still has a listed phone number.

The First Family of auto racing. From left, Bill, Jr.; Bill, Sr.; Anne and Jim.

"They're all competitors," he says. "If David and Richard were running side by side, and there wasn't the glory of winning and the pot of gold, I doubt if they'd run as hard as they do. I'd bet that if they got $25 an hour on a test track, they wouldn't run as hard."

But what about the talk of the current crop of NASCAR drivers getting old? Who will fill their places?

"A driver doesn't get obsolete in motorsports as soon as they do in other sports," France says. "Sure they have to be alert, and they have to have the desire to win, but age in a driver is probably to his advantage, because he has more experience.

"Over the years, we've had top name drivers who were older; it's usually been that way. And guys like Waltrip have been successful as newcomers, but not until they got their mechanical act together. He (Waltrip) might have been just as good all along, but he needed good equipment. Look at Ricky Rudd, or maybe Richard's boy (Kyle). There are probably more young guys standing in line to get a good ride today than there ever have been.

"There's no lack of talent coming along. It's there. They just have to wait until somebody backs off."

But somehow you can tell that the man who started it all knows that there aren't many Smokey Pursers or Red Byrons or Fireball Roberts' standing in lines anywhere. Or Curtis Turners. They were a breed all to themselves.

As I listened to this giant of auto racing, I couldn't help but remember something that Bill Robinson had written in the *Atlanta Journal* a long time ago:

"What could be more beautiful than Petty and Pearson, running flat out, Dixie-style, belly-to-the-ground, chasing a hurrying sundown."

Salute

The first time I met Bill France, Sr., I ended up having breakfast with him and Annie in their kitchen. He was just getting started then; Buck Baker was there—he drove a Corvette on the beach at 169 mph—this was the early '50s. . . . I forget just which year.

Harley Earl, head of all General Motors design, introduced us. I was a protege of Harley Earl, and followed Earl into the vice presidency of design when he retired.

When Bill had the Daytona International Speedway under construction, but not yet paved—he took me out in a Pontiac convertible, with the top down—and went 125 mph. Then he said, "You drive. . .take your hands off the wheel. . .it'll just stay up there." —and it did.

Bill was out to compete with Indy. He built the first high bank track in the country—the Indy cars couldn't handle it, but the Detroit-built stockers could. Then he went and built Talladega—a faster and steeper track. Bill wasn't out to run just one race a year, but NASCAR races all year 'round, nationally.

Bill has a good relationship with the automotive people; a great one with Bunkey Knudsen. . .actually helped make Knudsen when he was head of Pontiac. . .Pontiac won—and its popularity put Pontiac sales ahead of Buick and Oldsmobile in one year.

He had a fine relationship with Ed Cole, retired president of General Motors, until his death in a plane crash; and now with the present president of GM, Pete Estes. . .and Chuck Pilliod, chairman of the board of Goodyear, and Ue Shima, president of Yamaha, among others.

He's done a lot for the automotive industry, running stock, sports and Indy car races as well as the biggest motorcycle race in the world—each March at least fifteen charter flights, loaded with competitors from Sweden, Italy, Germany, England and more, all head to Daytona.

When Bill puts his mind to something he goes and does it—he has no patience with weak or ineffective people.

I like to think of him as the 'John Wayne' of racing, a rough man who plays square. . . .can't believe he's from Ohio—he's always seemed a Texan to me—as much a Texan as any man I've met.

Industry, enthusiasts and competitors salute Bill France, Sr., and thank him for what he has done.

Bill Mitchell
September 14, 1979

(ed. note: Bill Mitchell retired two years ago as vice president of design for General Motors. Presently he is a design consultant for Goodyear, 3M and Yamaha—and is an avid automobile and motorcycle race enthusiast who seldom misses a race.)

Daytona Records

Distance	Time	M.P.H.	Driver	Car	Date
		1903			
1 Kilo	32.80	68.198	Winton	Winton	Feb. 26
		1904			
1 Kilo	24.40	84.731	Basle	Mercedes	Feb. 1
		Equalled world record of Duray at Dourdan			
1 Mile	39.00	92.307	Vanderbilt	Mercedes	Jan. 27
5 Mile	3:31.20	85.207	Vanderbilt	Mercedes	Jan. 29
10 Mile	6:50.00	87.805	Vanderbilt	Mercedes	Jan. 30
15 Mile	10:18.00	87.379	Bowden	Mercedes	Jan. 27
20 Mile	17:02.00	70.450	Vanderbilt	Mercedes	Jan. 30
30 Mile	24:11.00	74.431	Vanderbilt	Mercedes	Jan. 30
40 Mile	33:52.40	70.852	Vanderbilt	Mercedes	Jan. 30
50 Mile	40:49.80	73.402	Vanderbilt	Mercedes	Jan. 30
		1905			
1 Kilo	20.60	108.589	Bowden	Mercedes	Jan. 31
1 Mile	34.40	104.651	MacDonald	Napier	Jan. 25
1 Mile	32.80	109.756	Bowden	Mercedes	Jan. 25
5 Mile	3:17.00	91.371	MacDonald	Napier	Jan. 24
10 Mile	5:15.00	96.000	MacDonald	Napier	Jan. 31
20 Mile	13:20.00	90.000	Thomas	Mercedes	Jan. 31
30 Mile	20:27.00	88.020	Thomas	Mercedes	Jan. 31
40 Mile	31:54.40	75.219	Sartori	Fiat	Jan. 31
50 Mile	38:51.00	77.220	Fletcher	DeDietrich	Jan. 31
100 Mile	1:18:24.00	76.531	Fletcher	DeDietrich	Jan. 30
		1906			
1 Kilo	18.40	121.572	Marriott	Stanley	Jan. 26
1 Mile	28.20	127.659	Marriott	Stanley	Jan. 26
2 Mile	58.80	122.449	Demogeot	Darracq	Jan. 29
5 Mile	2:47.20	107.656	Marriott	Stanley	Jan. 24
15 Mile	10:00.00	90.000	Lancia	Fiat	Jan. 29
100 Mile	1:15:42.40	79.253	Cliffort-Earp	Napier	Jan. 27
		1908			
100 Mile	1:12:56.20	82.263	Bernin	Renault	Mar. 6
250 Mile	3:16:48.60	76.216	Cedrino	Fiat	Mar. 5
300 Mile	3:53:44.00	77.011	Cedrino	Fiat	Mar. 5
		1909			
5 Mile	2:45.20	108.956	Robertson	Benz	Mar. 24
10 Mile	5:14.20	114.500	Bruce-Brown	Benz	Mar. 24
100 Mile	1:12:45.20	82.470	Burman	Renault	
		1910			
1 Kilo	17.04	131.275	Oldfield	Benz	Mar. 23
1 Mile	27.33	131.724	Oldfield	Benz	Mar. 16
		1911			
1 Kilo	15.88	140.865	Burman	Benz	Apr. 23
1 Mile ss.	40.52	88.845	Oldfield	Benz	Mar. 28
1 Mile	25.40	141.732	Burman	Benz	Apr. 23
2 Mile	51.28	140.406	Burman	Benz	Apr. 23
20 Mile	13:11.92	90.918	Burman	Benz	Apr. 23

1919

1 Kilo	14.86	149.859	DePalma	Packard	Feb. 12
1 Mile ss.	38.83	92.713	DePalma	Packard	Feb. 17
1 Mile	24.02	149.875	DePalma	Packard	Feb. 12
2 Mile	49.54	145.337	DePalma	Packard	Feb. 16
3 Mile	1:15.04	143.923	DePalma	Packard	Feb. 16
4 Mile	1:39.77	144.332	DePalma	Packard	Feb. 16
5 Mile	2:04.58	144.485	DePalma	Packard	Feb. 16
10 Mile	4:09.60	148.409	DePalma	Packard	Feb. 16
15 Mile	6:48.75	132.110	DePalma	Packard	Feb. 17
20 Mile	8:54.20	134.789	DePalma	Packard	Feb. 17

1920

1/2 Mile	11.57	155.575	Milton	Duesenberg	Apr. 27
1 Kilo	14.40	155.342	Milton	Duesenberg	Apr. 27
1 Mile	23.07	156.046	Milton	Duesenberg	Apr. 27
2 Mile	46.42	155.709	Milton	Duesenberg	Apr. 27
3 Mile	1:12.18	149.626	Milton	Duesenberg	Apr. 25
4 Mile	1:36.14	149.782	Milton	Duesenberg	Apr. 25
5 Mile	2:00.04	149.950	Milton	Duesenberg	Apr. 25
Class "C":					
1 Kilo	18.22	122.773	Murphy	Duesenberg	Apr. 27
1 Mile	29.36	122.615	Murphy	Duesenberg	Apr. 27
5 Mile	2:29.14	120.691	Murphy	Duesenberg	Apr. 27

1922

1 Mile	19.97	180.270	Haugdahl	Wisconsin	Apr. 6

1927

1 Kilo	11.02	202.988	Segrave	Sunbeam	Mar. 29
1 Mile	17.65	203.792	Segrave	Sunbeam	Mar. 29
5 Mile	55.18	202.675	Segrave	Sunbeam	Mar. 29

1928

1 Mile	17.39	206.956	Campbell	Napier	Feb. 19
1 Mile	17.34	207.552	Keech	White	Apr. 22
Class "D":					
1 Mile	18.15	198.292	Lockhart	Stutz	Apr. 25

1929

1 Kilo	9.66	231.447	Segrave	Napier	Mar. 11
1 Mile	15.56	231.362	Segrave	Napier	Mar. 11

1931

1 Kilo	9.09	246.086	Campbell	Napier	Feb. 5
1 Mile	14.65	245.733	Campbell	Napier	Feb. 5

1932

1 Kilo	8.90	251.340	Campbell	Napier	Feb. 24
1 Mile	14.17	253.968	Campbell	Napier	Feb. 24
5 Kilo	46.30	241.569	Campbell	Napier	Feb. 24
5 Kilo	45.11	247.941	Campbell	Napier	Feb. 26
5 Mile	1:14.15	242.751	Campbell	Napier	Feb. 26
10 Kilo	1:33.72	238.669	Campbell	Napier	Feb. 26

1933

1 Kilo	8.21	273.432	Campbell	Rolls-Royce	Feb. 22
1 Mile	13.23	272.108	Campbell	Rolls-Royce	Feb. 22

| 5 Kilo | 43.47 | 257.295 | Campbell | Rolls-Royce | Feb. 22 |

1935

| 1 Mile | 13.01 | 276.820 | Campbell | Rolls-Royce | Mar. 7 |

Daytona 200 Motorcycle Race (Beach Course)

Year	Driver	Car	M.P.H.
1937	Ed Kretz	Indian	37.34
1938	Ben Campanale	Harley-Davidson	73.99
1939	Ben Campanale	Harley-Davidson	76.88
1940	Babe Tancrede	Harley-Davidson	75.11
1941	Billy Mathews	Norton	78.08
1947	Johnny Splegelhoff	Indian	77.14
1948	Floyd Emde	Indian	74.01
1949	Dick Klamfoth	Norton	86.42
1950	Billy Mathews	Norton	88.55
1951	Dick Klamfoth	Norton	92.81
1952	Dick Klamfoth	Norton	87.91
1953	Paul Goldsmith	Harley-Davidson	94.25
1954	Bobby Hill	BSA	94.25
1955	Brad Andres	Harley-Davidson	94.57
1956	John Gibson	Harley-Davidson	94.21
1957	Joe Leonard	Harley-Davidson	98.52
1958	Joe Leonard	Harley-Davidson	99.86
1959	Brad Andres	Harley-Davidson	98.70
1960	Brad Andres	Harley-Davidson	98.06

Daytona 200 Motorcycle Race (Speedway)

Year	Driver	Car	M.P.H.
1961	Roger Reiman	Harley-Davidson	69.25
1962	Don Burnett	Triumph	71.98
1963	Ralph White	Harley-Davidson	77.67
1964	Roger Reiman	Harley-Davidson	94.83
1965	Roger Reiman	Harley-Davidson	90.04
1966	Buddy Elmore	Triumph	96.58
1967	Gary Nixon	Truimph	98.22
1968	Calvin Rayborn	Harley-Davidson	101.29
1969	Calvin Rayborn	Harley-Davidson	100.88
1970	Dick Mann	Honda	102.69
1971	Dick Mann	BSA	104.73
1972	Don Emde	Yamaha	103.35
1973	Jarno Saarinen	Yamaha	98.17
1974	Giacomo Agostini	Yamaha	105.01
1975	Gene Romero	Yamaha	106.45
1976	Johnny Cecotto	Yamaha	108.77
1977	Steve Baker	Yamaha	108.85
1978	Kenny Roberts	Yamaha	108.37

Beach Course (Prior to NASCAR)

Year	Driver	Car	M.P.H.
1936	Milt Marion	Ford	52.21
1937	Smokey Purser	Ford	67.00
1938	Bill France	Ford	*

1938	Danny Murphy **	Ford	68.66
1939	Sam Rice	Mercury	70.34
1939	Stuart Joyce	Ford	76.03
1940	Rod Hall	Ford	76.53
1940	Bill France	Buick	75.00
1941	Rod Hall	Ford	75.00
1941	Smokey Purser	Ford	76.19
1946	Red Byron	Ford	80.20
1947	Red Bryon	Ford	77.40

* Purser disqualified, no speed recorded on second place car.
** Two races each year between 1938 and 1941

Beach Course (NASCAR)

Year	Driver	Car	M.P.H.
1948	Red Byron	'39 Ford	75.94
1949	Red Byron	'49 Olds 88	79.26
1950	Harold Kite	'49 Lincoln	81.75
1951	Marshall Teague	'51 Hudson	82.39
1952	Marshall Teague	'52 Hudson	84.65
1953	Bill Blair	'53 Olds 88	89.50
1954	Lee Petty	'54 Chrysler	89.14
1955	Tim Flock	'55 Chrysler	92.05
1956	Tim Flock	'56 Chry. 300	90.83
1957	Cotton Owens	'57 Pontiac	101.60
1958	Paul Goldsmith	'58 Pontiac	101.18

Convertible Races

Year	Driver	Car	M.P.H.
1956	Curtis Turner	'56 Ford	96.11
1957	Tim Flock	'57 Mercury	101.32
1958	Curtis Turner	'58 Ford	98.56

Beach Course (Modifieds)

Year	Driver	Car	M.P.H.
1949	Marshall Teague	'39 Ford	88.23
1950	Gober Soebee	'39 Ford	93.19
1951	Gober Soebee	'37 Ford	82.37
1952*	Jack Smith	'39 Ford	87.39
1953*	Cotton Owens	'38 Plymouth	91.54
1954	Cotton Ownes	'38 Plymouth	93.87
1955	Banjo Matthews	'40 Ford	98.24
1956*	Tim Flock	'39 Chevrolet	89.41
1957*	Speedy Thompson	'52 Plymouth	99.09
1958*	Banjo Matthews	'55 Ford	97.38

Sportsman

Year	Driver	Car	M.P.H.
1954	Dick Joslin	'39 Ford	87.92
1955	Speedy Thompson	'40 Ford	89.52

* Combined Modified/Sportsman races

Continental/24 Hours of Daytona

Year	Driver	Car	M.P.H.
1962	Dan Gurney	Lotus 19	104.10
1963	Pedro Rodriguez	Ferrari	102.07
1964	Pedro Rodriguez	Ferrari	98.23
1965	Miles/Ruby	Ford prototype	99.94
1966*	Miles/Ruby	Ford Mark II	108.02
1967	Bandini/Amon	Ferrari	105.68
1968	Elfort/Neerpasch	Porsche	106.69
1968	Sieffert/Stommelen	Porsche	106.69
1968	Hermann	Porsche	106.69
1969	Donohue/Parsons	Lola Chevy	99.26
1970	Rodriguez/Kinnunen	Porsche	114.86
1971	Rodriguez/Oliver	Porsche	109.20
1972**	Andretti/Ickx	Ferrari	122.57
1973	Gregg/Haywood	Porsche	106.22
1975	Gregg/Haywood	Porsche	108.53
1976	Gregg/Redman/Fitzpatrick	BMW	104.04
1977	Graves/Haywood/Helmick	Porsche	108.80
1978	Stommelen/Hezemans/Gregg	Porsche	108.74
1979	Ongais/Field/Haywood	Porsche	109.24

* Changed to 24 hours
** Six hour race in 1972
No race in 1974, energy crisis

Camel GT Challenge (IMSA)

Year	Driver	Car	M.P.H.
1971	Yenko/Heinz	Corvette	107.53
1972	*Kemp/Pickett	Corvette	105.76
1972	Gene Felton	Camaro	98.98
1973	*Gregg/Haywood	Porsche	109.02
1973	Hurley Haywood	Porsche	112.16
1974	John Greenwood	Corvette	115.65
1975	John Greewood	Corvette	116.77
1976	Michael Keyser	Monza	116.17
1977	Hurley Haywood	Porsche	114.23
1978	Gregg/Ongais/Paul	Porsche	117.86
1978	**Gene Felton	Buick Skyhawk	100.20

* Starlight Camel Challenge
** Champion Spark Plug Challenge

Firecracker 250/400 Winners

Year	Driver	Car	M.P.H.
1959	Fireball Roberts	Pontiac	140.581
1960	Jack Smith	Pontiac	146.842
1961	David Pearson	Pontiac	154.294
1962	Fireball Roberts	Pontiac	153.688
1963*	Fireball Roberts	Ford	150.927
1964	A. J. Foyt	Dodge	151.451
1965	A. J. Foyt	Ford	150.046
1966	Sam McQuagg	Dodge	153.813

1967	Cale Yarborough	Ford	143.583
1968	Cale Yarborough	Mercury	167.247
1969	Lee Roy Yarbrough	Ford	160.875
1970	Donnie Allison	Ford	162.235
1971	Bobby Isaac	Dodge	161.947
1972	David Pearson	Mercury	160.821
1973	David Pearson	Mercury	158.468
1974	David Pearson	Mercury	138.301
1975	Richard Petty	Dodge	158.381
1976	Cale Yarborough	Chevrolet	160.966
1977	Richard Petty	Dodge	142.716
1978	David Pearson	Mercury	154.340

* Race changed from 250 miles to 400 miles

February Daytona Sportsman Winners (ARCA)

Year	Driver	Car	M.P.H.
1959	Banjo Matthews	Ford	134.655
1960	Bubba Farr	Ford	116.612
1961	Jimmy Thompson	Ford	141.667
1962	Lee Roy Yarbrough	Ford	146.723
1963	Lee Roy Yarbrough	Studebaker	147.010
1964	Tiny Lund	Ford	104.506
1965	Marvin Panch	Ford	129.533
1966	Curtis Turner	Ford	144.520
1967	Jim Paschal	Plymouth	148.188
1968	Bunkie Blackburn	Dodge	140.432
1969	Lee Roy Yarbrough	Ford	105.365
1970	Tiny Lund	Ford	133.327
1971	Red Farmer	Ford	140.936
1972	Bill Dennis	Mercury	135.627
1973	Bill Dennis	Mercury	134.161
1974	Bill Dennis	Mercury	140.462
1975	Jack Ingram	Chevrolet	138.107
1976	Joe Millikan	Dodge	145.928
1977	Donnie Allison	Chevrolet	154.396
1978	Darrell Waltrip	Chevrolet	162.675
1979	Kyle Petty	Dodge	131.964

Daytona NASCAR 200 Modified Race

Year	Driver	Car	M.P.H.
1974	Bobby Allison	Camaro	98.879
1975	Merv Treichler	Monza	99.407
1976	Bobby Allison	Hornet	105.730
1977	Harry Gant	Firebird	136.132
1978	Darrell Waltrip	Camaro	134.831

Daytona 500 Qualifying Races

Year	Driver	Car	M.P.H.
1959	Shorty Rollins	Ford	129.50
1959	Bob Welborn	Chevrolet	143.198
1960	Fireball Roberts	Pontiac	137.614

1960	Jack Smith	Pontiac	146.520
1961	Fireball Roberts	Pontiac	133.037
1961	Joe Weatherly	Pontiac	152.607
1962	Fireball Roberts	Pontiac	156.999
1962	Joe Weatherly	Pontiac	145.395
1963	Junior Johnson	Chevrolet	164.083
1963	Johnny Rutherford	Chevrolet	162.969
1964	Junior Johnson	Dodge	170.777
1964	Bobby Isaac	Dodge	169.811
1965	Darel Dieringer	Mercury	165.669
1965	Junior Johnson	Ford	111.076
1966	Paul Goldsmith	Plymouth	167.988
1966	Earl Balmer	Dodge	153.256
1967	Lee Roy Yarbrough	Dodge	163.934
1967	Fred Lorenzen	Ford	174.583
1969*	David Pearson	Ford	152.181
1969*	Bobby Isaac	Dodge	151.668
1970	Cale Yarborough	Mercury	183.295
1970	Charlie Glotzbach	Dodge	147.734
1971	Pete Hamilton	Plymouth	175.029
1971	David Pearson	Mercury	168.728
1972	Bobby Isaac	Dodge	127.118
1972	Bobby Allison	Chevrolet	178.217
1973	Buddy Baker	Dodge	173.611
1973	Coo Coo Marlin	Chevrolet	157.177
1974	Bobby Isaac	Chevrolet	123.212
1974	Cale Yarborough	Chevrolet	129.724
1975	Bobby Allison	Matador	156.685
1975	David Pearson	Mercury	156.958
1976	Dave Marcus	Dodge	119.458
1976	Darrell Waltrip	Chevrolet	156.250
1977	Richard Petty	Dodge	179.856
1977	Cale Yarborough	Chevrolet	171.429
1978	A. J. Foyt	Buick	123.018
1978	Darrel Waltrip	Chevrolet	169.683
1979	Buddy Baker	Olds	167.598
1979	Darrell Waltrip	Chevrolet	153.009

1968—no qualifying races due to rain
* Races changed from 100 miles to 125 miles

Daytona 500 Winner

Year	Driver	Car	M.P.H.
1959	Lee Petty	Olds 88	135.521
1960	Junior Johnson	Chevrolet	124.740
1961	Marvin Panch	Pontiac	149.601
1962	Fireball Roberts	Pontiac	152.529
1963	Tiny Lund	Ford	151.566
1964	Richard Petty	Plymouth	154.334
1965*	Fred Lorenzen	Ford	141.539
1966**	Richard Petty	Plymouth	160.627
1967	Mario Andretti	Ford	146.926
1968	Cale Yarborough	Mercury	143.251
1969	Lee Roy Yarbrough	Ford	157.950
1970	Pete Hamilton	Plymouth	149.601
1971	Richard Petty	Plymouth	144.462
1972	A. J. Foyt	Mercury	161.550

1973	Richard Petty	Dodge	157.205
1974***	Richard Petty	Dodge	140.894
1975	Benny Parsons	Chevrolet	153.649
1976	David Pearson	Mercury	152.181
1977	Cale Yarborough	Chevrolet	153.218
1978	Bobby Allison	Ford	159.730
1979	Richard Petty	Olds	143.977

*   332½ miles because of rain
**   495 miles because of rain
*** 450 miles because of fuel shortage

All Time NASCAR Standings

(Through 1978)

Driver	Wins	Races	Money Earned
1. Richard Petty	185	774	$3,102,485
2. Cale Yarborough	59	373	2,417,587
3. David Pearson	103	509	2,058,046
4. Bobby Allison	51	435	1,812,481
5. Buddy Baker	13	474	1,413,261
6. Benny Parsons	12	294	1,353,581
7. Darrell Waltrip	15	158	1,011,142
8. Dave Marcis	4	309	831,154
9. James Hylton	2	473	805,851
10. Donnie Allison	10	184	717,623
11. Dick Brooks	1	237	653,321
12. Bobby Isaac**	37	308	585,897
13. Cecil Gordon	0	355	567,641
14. J. D. McDuffie	0	410	490,829
15. Fred Lorenzen*	26	159	475,913
16. Lennie Pond	1	141	471,130
17. Lee Roy Yarbrough*	14	198	450,679
18. Richard Childress	0	202	448,723
19. Frank Warren	0	360	438,614
20. Buddy Arrington	0	303	430,904

* Retired
**Deceased

NASCAR Superspeedway Standings

(Through 1978)

Driver	Wins	Poles	Races	Money Earned
1. Richard Petty	44	26	267	$1,983,068
2. David Pearson	49	57	241	1,752,286
3. Cale Yarborough	29	27	207	1,551,982
4. Bobby Allison	26	18	225	1,328,819
5. Buddy Baker	12	15	232	1,189,299
6. Benny Parsons	7	2	175	894,368
7. Donnie Allison	9	13	139	661,268
8. Darrell Waltrip	6	2	109	655,044
9. Dave Marcis	2	9	176	562,167
10. James Hylton	1	0	210	495,230
11. Dick Brooks	1	0	152	489,107

12. Bobby Isaac**	3	9	135	410,072
13. Fred Lorenzen*	12	15	86	398,620
14. Lee Roy Yarbrough*	10	5	96	394,305
15. A. J. Foyt	7	9	70	377,640
16. Cecil Gordon	0	0	183	357,621
17. Lennie Pond	1	0	95	334,280
18. J. D. McDuffie	0	1	182	333,660
19. Frank Warren	0	0	196	320,310
20. Richard Chidress	0	0	123	294,253

* Retired
**Deceased

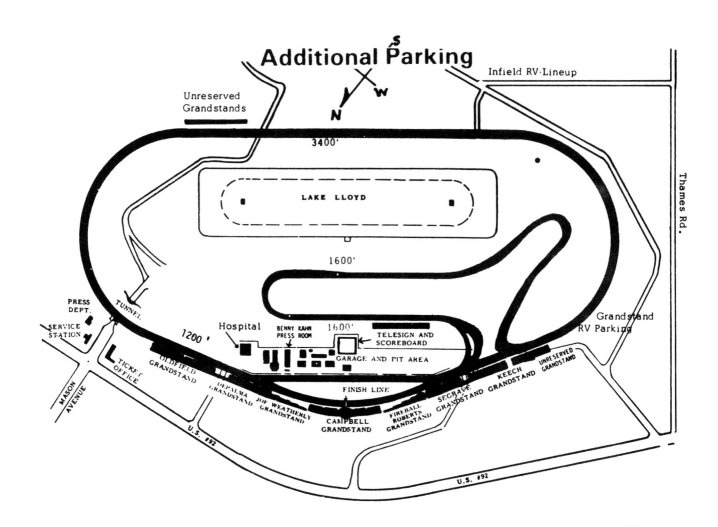

Driver Ranking per Money Won—Daytona International Speedway

(From 1959 Season through Firecracker 400, July 4, 1979, per NASCAR payout)

Driver	No. of Races	Best Fin.	Pct. Win	Avg. Fin.	Top 5	Top 10	Avg. Money Won	Total Money Won
Richard Petty	38	1-(8)	.2105	11.76	18	24	$ 11,761.05	$446,920.00
Cale Yarborough	30	1-(5)	.1666	18.10	12	14	10,707.91	321,237.50
David Pearson	36	1-(6)	.1666	12.58	16	23	6,648.91	239,361.00
A.J. Foyt	28	1-(3)	.1071	17.07	10	12	7,187.50	201,250.00
Benny Parsons	20	1	.0500	14.20	8	11	9,981.05	199,621.00
Buddy Baker	34	2-(5)	.0000	19.85	10	13	5,857.57	199,157.50
Bobby Allison	31	1	.0322	17.80	8	10	5,916.29	183,405.00
Darrell Waltrip	14	2-(2)	.0000	15.35	5	7	11,294.50	158,123.00
Donnie Allison	21	1	.0476	17.42	6	10	6,048.57	127,020.00
Lee Roy Yarbrough	16	1-(2)	.1250	14.68	4	8	6,265.00	100,240.00
Richard Brooks	19	3	.0000	15.57	3	11	5,031.84	95,605.00
Fred Lorenzen	16	1	.0625	10.18	10	12	5,809.37	92,950.00
Dave Marcis	22	3	.0000	16.45	2	8	4,135.13	90,995.00
Bobby Isaac	20	1	.0500	16.05	5	10	3,987.75	79,755.00
Coo Coo Marlin	21	4-(3)	.0000	22.09	3	5	3,641.19	76,465.00
Frank Warren	27	10-(2)	.0000	19.44	0	2	2,735.33	73,854.00
James Hylton	25	3	.0000	14.88	3	13	2,759.80	68,995.00
Neil Bonnett	8	1	.1250	20.75	2	3	7,600.62	60,805.00
J.D. McDuffie	22	7	.0000	25.27	0	1	2,548.86	56,075.00
Fireball Roberts	11	1-(4)	.2857	20.00	5	5	5,072.73	55,800.00

Total No. of Races—42   Avg. Payout Per Race—$127,238.14

Total No. of Entries—1,782   Avg. Payout Per Entry—$2,998.87

Total Payout—$5,344,002

NASCAR **Winston Cup Grand National**

Car Ranking per. Money Won—Daytona International Speedway

(From 1959 Season through Firecracker 400, July 4, 1979, per NASCAR payout)

Make	Entries	Wins	Running	Pct. Running	Out Via Accident	Pct. Accident	Avg. Money Won	Total Money Won
Chevrolet	516	4	247	47.86	25	4.84	$2,733.70	$1,410,591.00
Ford	471	10	235	49.89	32	6.79	2,137.72	1,006,867.00
Dodge	273	7	138	50.54	24	8.79	3,312.60	904,342.00
Oldsmobile	66	2	30	45.45	7	10.60	9,258.10	611,035.00
Mercury	131	9	74	56.48	13	9.92	4,337.18	568,171.00
Plymouth	132	4	76	57.57	5	3.78	2,953.52	389,865.00
Pontiac	123	6	59	47.96	2	1.62	1,731.66	212,995.00
Buick	27	0	11	40.74	6	22.22	6,075.74	164,045.00
Matador	8	0	4	50.00	0	.00	5,866.87	46,935.00
Thunderbird	20	0	16	80.00	1	5.00	1,201.00	24,020.00
Chrysler	12	0	4	33.33	1	8.30	402.08	4,825.00
Studebaker	1	0	1	100.00	0	.00	110.00	110.00
Desoto	1	0	0	.00	0	.00	100.00	100.00
Edsel	1	0	0	.00	0	.00	100.00	100.00
Total	1782	42	895	50.22	116	6.50	$2,998.87	$5,344,002.00

Autographs

Autographs

Autographs

Autographs

NASCAR Membership:

For information on how to become a member of NASCAR, either competitive or non-competitive, and receive the NASCAR newsletter as well as other information, write to: National Association for Stock Car Auto Racing, Inc., P O Box K, Daytona Beach, Florida 32015.

AZTEX Corporation—Research Information

This book is part of a continuing research project. Please advise us of any additions or corrections which you may come across in reading this volume. Any picture or other material which you feel should be considered for inclusion in a future edition may be sent to the editor. If you want your material to be returned please enclose a stamped, self-addressed envelope with the correct postage. The material will be copied and placed in our file for consideration. Any information, no matter how obscure or seemingly unimportant, is welcomed. In sending information, please make reference to the title and author and mail to: Editor, AZTEX Corporation, P O Box 50046, Tucson, Arizona 85703.